...how one single girl got married

Quadrille

Dedication

For Nirpal Singh Dhaliwal

First published in 2005 by
Quadrille Publishing Limited
Alhambra House
27-31 Charing Cross Road,
London WC2H OLS

Reprinted in 2005
10 9 8 7 6 5 4 3 2

Editorial Director Jane O'Shea
Art Director Helen Lewis
Editor Nicki Marshall
Designer Ros Holder
Production Rebecca Short

Cover illustration by Bee Murphy

Text © 2005 Liz Jones
Design & layout © 2005 Quadrille Publishing Ltd

Cataloguing in Publication Data: a catalogue record for this book is available from
the British Library

HARDBACK ISBN: 1 84400 223 3
Printed in China

Liz Jones's Diary...

CONTENTS

PART ONE

Single file

Introduction

YOU DON'T HAVE MALE

First of all, let me point out that I am not a dating expert. Far from it. I have had very few boyfriends; in fact, I could count them on the fingers of one hand, without any need for the thumb. I think, looking back, that only one man has ever actually asked me out, and I got so excited I married him. The others – all three of them – sort of meandered around, vaguely hinting we might one day go to see a movie, and then wandered off again, muttering, 'I'm not really ready for a relationship.'

I have, on many occasions, asked myself why this should be the case. After all, you see plenty of not particularly attractive women with outgrowing roots and fairly decent husbands, leading normal lives. They, I am quite sure, didn't spend literally decades in the dating wilderness, waiting for the phone to ring.

There are several main reasons why I didn't ever have much interest from men.

1. I was, and am, painfully shy. Couple this with the fact I only took up drinking (organic vegan wine) on Millennium Eve (of which more later), and that I have never taken drugs or smoked, and the result was I was always too terrified of boys to go anywhere near them. If I liked someone, I would generally ignore him.

2. I set my sights ridiculously high. In strict chronological order, I have tried to engineer, quite seriously, to go out with:

Paul Newman

Davy Jones

Paul McCartney

Jan Michael Vincent (the early days)

Ben Murphy

David Cassidy

Marc Bolan

Mickey Rourke (circa *Diner*)

Andrew McCarthy (still; please call me)

Adam Ant (very nice cheekbones; don't like him now, though)

Bruce Willis (circa *Moonlighting*)

Patrick Swayze (circa *North and South* and *Point Break*)

Jim Kerr

Prince

Keanu Reeves (circa *Point Break*)

Justin Timberlake (very bendy; not that keen on his hair, though)

None of these men reciprocated my feelings. You might say we were never given a chance because we never met, but that would be untrue. I have, for the record, met six of the above. Needless to say, there wasn't even a hint of a spark on their part and I came away very disappointed indeed.

3. Mobile phones and email hadn't, for most of my dating career, been invented. This is a shame, as I am sure that had I been able to email or text-message some of the men who have crossed my path, therefore neatly sidestepping problem number 1, we would have had a lot more progress.

4. Fashion designers. They really do have a lot to answer for in my case, bearing in mind that I have, neatly piled upstairs, every copy of *Vogue* since September 1977, when it came out twice a year and cost just 50p. At various times since purchasing that fateful first copy, I have worn no make-up and sported white rags tied in my hair and long, voluminous skirts (it was a sort of prairie look with lots of broderie anglaise by designers like Body Map and Margaret Howell – this was 1981, when a rather plain model, photographed

by Barry Lategan, was the epitome of beauty). I then aspired to look like American model Janice Dickinson. My favourite *Vogue* cover of all time is from August 1982, and features Janice, all Galaxy Counter eyes and rosebud mouth, olive skin and Brooke Shields eyebrows. Her sister, Sandra, was also a model. An image that springs to mind is from *Beauty in Vogue* – a separate magazine published mid-month – in which Sandra was photographed on a yacht in the sunshine wearing white shorts and eating a watermelon; I have aspired to do that ever since.

I spent most of the eighties in black Lycra leggings, wearing leg-warmers on my ankles and arms, cropped tops – merely sweatshirts that I chopped in half – bought from Pineapple in Covent Garden, and with Molton Browners in my hair (bendy bits of wire covered in foam that gave me curls just like Andie Macdowell's on the cover of *Harpers & Queen*; I wasn't fond of the Rosie Velas or the Christie Brinkleys or the Jerry Halls – I preferred dark girls like me who probably had several pots of Jolen Creme Bleach stashed in their knicker drawers).

Since then, there have been Donna Karan bodies with poppers that brought tears to my eyes; batwing Lurex sweaters that knocked over all and sundry; denim jumpsuits that resulted in one quite embarrassing incident on a long journey; sweater dresses that, as soon as you sat down, began to sag at the bottom; stonewashed jeans with rips at the buttock and knee, with black Wolford tights worn underneath (my Bros period); a brown Katharine Hamnett dress that kept riding up; green Calvin Klein shorts worn with a gold Katharine Hamnett waistcoat, prompting one boy at a disco to remark that I looked like a circus entertainer; various items from Joseph; lots of outfits from Dirk Bikkembergs that needed a jolly good iron; low-slung combat pants worn with Timberland boots (my All Saints period); various hipster trouser suits from Helmut Lang which, although flattering, and which I still favour as my 'office uniform', The Husband has just informed me mark me out most definitely as a lesbian. We haven't even started on the high street, which I discovered only recently after accidentally walking into Topshop on Kensington High Street. I came away with a tiny tweed jacket that has arms that are too short, and some vintage shoes from Saxone that give me blisters. Trust me: on the whole, I didn't always have a great look.

5. I had, and still have, a tendency to try too hard, putting a great deal of pressure on my potential date/boyfriend/husband. I used to live next door to a man named David Scrace, or 'Scarce' as he soon became known. I was renting a house in Stockwell, south London, with my older sister Sue, and David lived next door with a pack of boys who were, I'm convinced, the prototype for the TV series *The Young Ones*. I don't know what it was about David that made me fall in love with him, because he never once gave me any encouragement, but I did, completely. He was very thin, with small, round teddy-bear eyes like Jim Kerr's, and a little rat's tail plait at the back of his head. He worked for Dunhill in Piccadilly – something in advertising – and came from up north. I embarked on a two-year campaign to get him to go out with me, which resulted in absolutely bloody zilch. I decorated the front door wearing knickers and a Frankie Say Relax T-shirt [sic] so that he would see me as he went in and out. He didn't bat an eyelid, merely asking me to do his windowsill as well. He said he liked to play squash, so I volunteered to be his partner, despite never having played in my life. I went on a crash course and bought all the kit but, of course, straight after our game he announced he was going out to dinner with a Malaysian girl, and could I take his racket home and leave it on the doorstep?

I bought him a duvet cover – black and white stripes – for his birthday. When he said he had helped to compile *The Sloane Ranger's Handbook*, I told him I worked on *Harpers & Queen* (I didn't; I worked on *Company* magazine, although I will say in my defence that they were on the same floor). I learned to drive and bought a red Mini City so that I could offer him lifts (I took my test twice; I failed the first one for 'driving too close to pedestrians'). My campaign culminated in my hosting a party so that I could invite him. I filled my washing machine with Pimm's, made fruit salad, warmed croissants and hired a DJ who played all those records with scratching and talking on them (this was 1983, the era of rap and 'Thriller'). David came to the party and immediately got off with my friend Wilma, who had turned up in an old frock and probably hadn't even washed.

Thus, I learned a lesson that holds true to this day: that the world is divided into two types of women. There are those who never have to try and who are really demanding and need picking up and buying dinner and into whose laps men just seemingly drop. (My friend Jenni is one of these; she once went out with a man just so that he would dispose of a lump of concrete in front of her house. She has just started seeing someone, but he hasn't been allowed to kiss her yet, and she doesn't like his name, so she is already calling him something else. 'He doesn't mind,' she says sweetly.) And then there are women like me, who have to cheat, change career, hire caterers and private detectives, learn new languages and take on new ethnicities, wait and generally orchestrate to even get noticed. I have never believed that I would meet someone when I am least expecting it. And if I ever do, I am sure I will be testing my tyre pressures while wearing stained tracky bottoms (very unflattering angle, lots of swearing).

After David, I fell in love with a young man who worked in a health-food store. After a year or so I had my very own peanut-butter mountain, but not a single date.

Next, I fancied a waiter, and spent a fortune taking all my girl-friends for dinner at the restaurant in Covent Garden where he worked. Nobody was allowed to complain about the food. I was devastated when I heard he had left to wait elsewhere, and so enlisted all my friends to keep their eyes peeled. At a drinks party, my friend Robina looked up from her canapé to see him holding a silver platter, and immediately rang me, saying she expected a finder's fee. I didn't go so far as holding my own party and hiring him to cater (although it did cross my mind) but I did persuade Jenni (of the concrete) to invite him to her 30th birthday bash on Brick Lane. He came, and stood chatting with his mate all evening, drinking beer. He didn't speak to me once.

I did manage to cultivate two boyfriends prior to meeting The Man I Was In Love With, closely followed by my future husband (there was one glorious weekend when I actually double parked). The first, Mad Richard, lasted six months and was, I have to admit, a complete disaster. He didn't phone me for weeks on end (even now, the recorded message, 'Sorry, the Vodafone you are calling may be switched off', sends shivers down my spine) and when he did call it was chaos. I still can't believe I lost my virginity in a flat in Lewisham, in a rancid bed that, to my horror, contained a long-past-its-sell-by-date packet of Tuc biscuits.

Boyfriend Number Two, Trevor, always maintained he was 'not in a relationship' even though we went out for about a decade and he actually lived with me from 1990 until I got Snoopy, which, according to his inoculation card (Snoopy's, not Trevor's) was September 1993. Abiding memories of Trevor include me giving him lifts to Holborn Tube station in my ancient Beetle, him making mixed tapes on my Technics stereo, and Herculean efforts on my part to keep the relationship going. How many times did I heave enormous bags of Marks & Spencer ready meals home after work to make him a nice supper? How many freebie CDs did I call in for him from the record companies at work? I was always buying him gifts – record decks, sound mixers, Smedley sweaters, a really nice dressing gown – but got very little in return; a giant, appliquéd card was about the sum of it. I became quite bitter, actually. Even after he moved out, we still dated (I mean that in the American sense; we didn't actually have sex as he was by then living with a stylist named Jenny, half my age, height and intellect). I realised it was finally over when, out for dinner with Trevor come a quarter to ten, I was looking at my watch and thinking, Can I get home in time for *ER*?

Do men know that women have these mad, all-consuming crushes on them, and go to bizarre lengths to get noticed? If all these men I was in love with did guess, it was very mean of them not to tell me they weren't interested/already had a girlfriend/were secretly gay. They would have saved me several years of Pilates classes. I remember sitting next to David Scrace in a pub off Acre Lane and him feeling my thigh and saying, 'Goodness, aren't your legs smooth?' And inside I was screaming, Yes, they're waxed because of you, they are always waxed just in case you notice me putting out the rubbish in my needlecord hot pants! (Years later, in about 2000, a friend of his phoned me at work to say that David was now divorced, and had a son at Westminster public school. Quite a large part of me was tempted to start my campaign afresh.)

6. Finally, I have never made friends easily. I have Jeremy and Kerry, and Emine and Robi, and now Harriet and Sue Needleman and Leggy and Bev. Meena and India I count as friends. But where-

as The Husband can bond with someone over yoga (his new gay best friend, Chris) or with Julie Burchill after meeting her, through me, just once (she gave him a Christmas present and card), I never think I am worth getting to know. I never know what to say at parties. I worry I am boring. Not clever enough. So the thought of someone finding me attractive AND interesting, well, that just ain't going to happen. Well, only once in a blue moon, and then he will find he has made a HIDEOUS mistake and run, screaming, for the hills.

You get the picture. There is an enormous amount of expectation on my part when I have even the hint of a romantic encounter. Take The Man I Was In Love With, Kevin. I met Kevin at the launch of Des'ree's second album. I was by this time working as a music writer on *The Sunday Times*, mainly so that I could meet Jim Kerr or Prince. Anyway, there he was: hair a mad whirl, like Osama Bin Laden's, in a shrunken stripy jumper, like one Dennis the Menace might wear. We started talking and that was it. I decided to track him down (my mantra over the years has always been, 'Would Madonna do this?' It has, occasionally, got me in to trouble). I got hold of his number and asked him to lunch at the restaurant where 'the waiter' was working; my plan was to make one or other of them jealous. I pretended I could give him work. He still didn't ask me out or phone me or show a flicker of interest, but I continued undaunted. I then became the editor of a glossy magazine and thought, Hurrah! I can hire him as the music critic, which I did, and EVENTUALLY, after about four million years and endless phone calls, he suggested we go to see a film. I had to ask my best friend Kerry whether or not this constituted a date, and she assured me it did, as it was a Sunday night. Hmmm. This is what I did prior to that all-important evening.

1. Hired a gardener to mow the lawn and mulch the flower-beds.

2. Asked my long-suffering and frequently ashen cleaner, H, to beeswax the floors.

3. Bought a new linen duvet cover from the Conran shop and ironed it with L'Occitane lavender water.

4. Bought two Diptyque candles.

5. Combed Snoopy and Squeaky, my two cats (of whom MUCH more later).

6. Had a leg and bikini wax (and, a few days later, an emergency knee wax).

7. Had my hair done with Aveda's top person, who only does supermodels and me.

8. Had an all-over St Tropez fake tan.

9. Had a deluxe pedicure.

10. Had my teeth cleaned by laser in Harley Street.

11. Booked the day off work.

12. Hosed my wheelie bin.

13. Went to see two new films so that I could be interesting.

The poor chap didn't stand much of a chance, did he? I met him outside the cinema in Russell Square and we went to see *The Blair Witch Project* followed by dinner at the Organic Pub, after which I dropped him off at his attic bedsit in Finsbury Park. I didn't even get a snog and I drove away in my Beetle at its top speed of 25 miles per hour really annoyed that, yet again, it had all come to nothing. I was so ready to have sex with him, everything had come together perfectly, and I knew that I wouldn't be as ready again for some time, what with re-growth and so forth; my optimum window for a date is as infrequent as a total eclipse of the sun.

Eventually, after much persuading and purchasing of buttery suede fringed trousers from Alberta Ferretti (I bought two pairs in case one developed a smudge), and probably without his knowledge, Kevin did in fact become Boyfriend Number Three. Which is how I came to be preparing to see him on Millennium Eve, the most important night of the century, dating wise. And thus began a fateful and often quite eventful five years. I have to point out here that everything you are about to read on the following pages is true, by the way, although I really, really wish it wasn't. Shall we begin?

FIRST, THOUGH, WE NEED A CAST OF CHARACTERS

ME. Thirtysomething former editor of a glossy magazine, now features editor on a daily newspaper, a job which is VERY, VERY stressful and tiring. Likes ponies, guinea pigs, cats, beauty products. Watches an enormous amount of TV. Not good in the morning. Was once told she resembles Madonna — but taller, and with brown eyes not blue, and without the gap in the teeth, obviously — which cheered her up for about a decade. Lives in Hackney, East London. Has only on one brief occasion been in credit at her bank; the manager actually phoned up so that she could hear the cheering. Has a tendency towards tidiness. Likes oily baths.

HUSBAND. Twenty-six when we met, about 5ft 10in, was 17 and a half stone but, having performed three hours of hot yoga each morning, including Sundays, for the past year, is now a trim 13. Has a close-shaved head and a stubbly beard, which can make it hard to determine which way up he is. Was born in Greenford (he would prefer 'mean streets of Southall' but that would be a lie) of immigrant Punjabi parents. Gained four As at A-level and got a degree at Nottingham University; can answer most of the questions on *University Challenge* (whereas his wife, to the question posed by Anne Robinson on *The Weakest Link*, 'What ancient form of preservation was practised by Inuits?' shouted, 'Jam!'). Is about to have his first novel published. Keeps striking possible poses for when he is famous and on the cover of *Vanity Fair*. Loves his cats. Very windy; often emits cabbagey smells.

SNOOPY. The original cat and, at 12, the oldest of what can only be described as a pack. Stripy with white paws. Very tolerant; hated Trevor (*see below*). Likes toes. I got him from a fashion designer acquaintance called Simon; I hadn't particularly wanted a kitten, merely to see inside Simon's flat and have the opportunity to call him over the years with updates. Likes pasta.

SQUEAKY. Cat number two, brought home by Snoopy as a rather rotund kitten. She is still very wide of girth and has been known to wear the cat flap as a skirt. Is black, which should be slimming. Can be depressed and prone to lash out. Dislikes stairs, jumping up, the garden. Likes to talk to me on the phone at work. Can only be bothered to wash her face. Very licky.

SUSAN. What can I say, she is a pocket-sized beauty, like a leopard: shy and brave and loving. Came from Celia Hammond's Animal Trust in Barking as a tiny, spitting kitten, totally feral, and it was a year before she would deign to be stroked. Likes to sleep curled, like a Catherine Wheel, on my chest. Likes prawns.

SWEETIE. Referred to by The Husband as 'my cat'; was abused as a baby and so has brain damage and a hare lip, but is so happy to live with us she can't stop purring; sniffs us very loudly. Also has Celia Hammond as her alma mater. Eats anything, including banana and cauliflower; was confused by peanut butter. Likes to motor round the lawn grunting.

RICHARD. Known as 'Mad Richard' for his propensity to drink vodka and go in to black moods. Has a tattoo. On a mini break in north Devon was unable to correctly identify a pigeon. Drives an old BMW.

TREVOR. Live-in boyfriend. Has a personality resembling Eeyore's and a vast collection of hip hop and Louis Farrakhan videos. Irons his trousers. Grew up in Ealing but now lives, I think, in Africa. Made me promise never to write about him. Still doesn't know how to drive. Not good with cats.

KEVIN. The Man I Was In Love With. About 32 when we met. He was working as a late-night radio DJ and was in a band; they actually made a record. Would sit on the floor and sing to me in a strangely deep voice. Resembles a young Gil Scott-Heron. Beautiful hands. Could, he assured me, have been a professional footballer were it not for his knee. Likes vintage sportswear.

JEREMY. Best Male Friend. We met in 1989 when we both worked on the now defunct magazine *Mirabella*. Lives in a loft and edits an interiors magazine. Used to be half of a power couple but now divorced. Wears immaculate suits and has been known to spend £400 on a jumper. Was scared of Mad Richard, disliked Trevor, never met Kevin but HEARD AN AWFUL LOT ABOUT HIM and thinks Husband needs a stern word.

KERRY. Best Female Friend. Very willing. Loyal. Was brought up in Hastings, so quite tough. Used to be a swimmer, now works on a national newspaper for 22 hours a day. Lives with Kevin (a different Kevin, otherwise she would no longer be Best Female Friend); used to live with Andy, a complete waste of space. Wears glasses. Pretends to do yoga twice a week. We met when I edited the glossy magazine. Was instrumental in getting me together with The Husband. Helped me organise the wedding, and very nearly came on our honeymoon.

ROBI. Very small, edits a magazine about shoes, is very keen to improve on her gene pool. Hasn't had a boyfriend for about two years. Likes chefs and thick tights. Suffers from a cat allergy.

DAVID. Husband's best friend, and indeed was his best man (his speech went on so long my mum fainted). Bad influence. Tall and handsome with a gold tooth. Lives with Danielle and rides a mountain bike. Always on the phone with The Husband. Doesn't have a land line. Secretly fancies me.

CHRISTOPHER SIRAGUSA. Okay, he is not really an issue over the next five years, because I didn't clap eyes on him after 1983, but he was a male model (Italian-American, with long dark hair and an amazing chest), and I did go out with him. We didn't have sex though; I thought he was shy, in retrospect I am sure he was gay. I interviewed him for *Company* magazine under a totally bogus pretext (we had lunch at Kettners in Soho) and I asked him to my house in Brixton for dinner. He turned up just as my sister Sue was on her way out for night duty at University College Hospital. She was in her uniform, complete with fob watch, belt and hat. 'Is she a nurse?' Christopher asked, puzzled. The best bit was when my neighbour saw him leaving the house and I felt really proud. I played poor unsuspecting Christopher the Simple Minds song 'Don't You Forget About Me' over and over again. He popped in to see me at work, and all the girls were goggle-eyed. We went for coffee and I mentioned Pinewood Studios had just burnt down. 'Oh no!' he exclaimed, almost in tears, 'All those trees!' I knew it was over when I rang on the doorbell of his top-floor flat in Knightsbridge and saw him look down out of the window at me, only for him not to let me in.

Chapter 1

MILLENNIUM EVE, EVE
HE GETS TO APPRECIATE MY BED LINEN

Hmmm. I am in Dolce and Gabbana on Old Bond Street trying to find SOMETHING to wear tomorrow night. I tell the male shop assistant what I am looking for and why. He looks slightly dubious, as I am still wearing a hair pack (similar to a face pack, but for the scalp); preparation for the big day has started early. He leads me to a pair of cream trousers encrusted with jewels. 'How much?' I squeak.

'£6,000.' I tell him the trousers are lovely but that I am looking for something full-length, not three-quarters. 'But that is what stops them being too classic,' he explains patiently. I would have thought the embroidered roses and milkmaids made of rubies would do that, but I make my excuses and head for Kookai, where I buy a pair of silver sequinned hipsters for forty quid.

I get home, and leave a message on Kevin's answer phone, inviting him for dinner the following night. I think he is my boyfriend, although I can't be one hundred per cent sure. After the abortive evening at *The Blair Witch Project*, he did, the following Friday, come round for dinner. He arrived, clasping an obscure jazz CD. I made him my signature dish: pasta with tomato sauce. We sat on my brand new Matthew Hilton chocolate-brown sofa, one each end. Eventually, he reached his hand out to mine and we sort of locked fingers. It was the most romantic moment I can remember, as spine-tingly exciting as when David Addison started rolling around on the floor with Maddie Hayes in *Moonlighting*, shouting, 'I'm tired of two years of "Is you is or is you ain't?"' We kissed. Thank God, he doesn't smell of Ralph Lauren's Polo (the aftershave of choice of Mad Richard). At last! I dragged him upstairs to the bedroom, for two reasons: 1. the sitting room was too bright; 2. I wanted him to appreciate my bed linen.

Sex was quite difficult at first; what can I say, the man had a certain girth. (This has happened to me once before, when I was 19 and had gone skiing in Montgeneve with my friend Sue Needleman – a Jewish princess with Southfork hair. I had got off with a boy called Michel, who washed up in one of the chalets – he had asked me what the words to the Bob Marley track 'Stir it up' meant, and I had mimed stirring a suet pudding – and we went down to the black, freezing hole that was my bedroom and he tried to get it in but he couldn't. I remember thinking it was a shame because I was seven and a half stone, and REALLY READY for a boyfriend; even a pen pal would have sufficed. It was many, many years before I dared try again. Sue Needleman still thinks I did it that night, by the way.)

Anyway, I digress. On that Friday night I had sex with Kevin, and he actually stayed until about 4 p.m. the next day, something of a record. There was a second night of passion about a week later, this time on the sofa, but he called a cab at midnight (I think his words were, 'I don't want people to think we're going out'; what people?), and then he phoned me when he got home and we talked till three in the morning. That was November. All in all, I thought I had a pretty good chance of a date on Millennium Eve.

MILLENNIUM EVE

It is now 7.30 p.m. Today I have had an oily bath, an Eve Lom Rescue Mask — mainly to counteract the effects of four hours' queuing in Sainsbury's — applied tinted moisturiser and copious amounts of Yves Saint Laurent Touche Eclat, given myself smoky eyes, adjusted the lighting, lit candles, consulted Kerry, opened the pasta sauce, and pulled apart a pillow of lamb's lettuce. He phones. He's not coming. I sound relaxed, not at all like this means I am going to have to watch *Dr Zhivago*, on my own, on the most crucial night of the century. He says he is going to the Embankment to watch the fireworks with his friend. I hope he falls into the Thames. He says, 'Why don't we have a drink before you go back to work?' It's a straw. I clutch at it.

MILLENNIUM EVE, BOXING DAY

I have gone into a decline.

Chapter 2

H e still hasn't called. For the first fortnight I'd constantly be listening out for the phone. I would check the landline for a dialling tone and I'd always have my mobile in the pocket of my tracky bottoms. Every time it rang, my heart would race and I would shove Lauryn Hill's 'Turn the Lights Down Low' on the turntable. In the third week this had become Marvin Gaye's 'Distant Lover'. By week four, the background music became Kelis's 'I Hate You So Much Right Now'.

I am writing this on a Thursday afternoon and, if I'm honest, do I really want him to call saying he 'might swing by'? I would have to leave work in time to go to M&S, which would probably give me plastic bag fingers, then buy flowers from McQueens (I think they are starting to get the gist of when I have a date, and now clap when I appear), get home and change the sheets and hide my Adam Ant records and have a bath and wash my hair and on and on and on. It's all so unbelievably tiring. If he doesn't call, I can meander home, watch *Friends* and *Frasier* and go to bed with a copy of *120 Ways to Make Your Cat Adore You* (a fabulous read, by the way. It says you should always bring a gift home for your cat, however small: an oak leaf, say; cats love new things).

My little friend Robi has kindly pointed out that if I keep writing about not having a boyfriend, I will never get another date as long as I live. Unless, of course, I go out with someone who can't read, which at this point is not something I am ruling out.

Perhaps I have been too fussy. I turned against Mad Richard not because he never returned my calls, but because the hi-fi in his car sounded tinny. Last week, I went to a party in the Hackney loft of a photographer friend of mine and met a man who tried to persuade me to go home with him. 'Why not? We can just talk, and I need someone to split the cab fare to Lewisham with me.' Charming. But I have my standards.

Because I am so pernickety, I'd prefer not to date a man who eats meat (perverse, I know, as Squeaky eats dolphin-friendly tuna and I let her lick my face), so this narrows my options somewhat. I'm still holding a torch for Kevin, even though he has been known to eat chicken, and am keeping up the maintenance just in case. I've had my legs waxed for the first time since the New Year's Eve debacle. I arrived at the beauty salon and the receptionist chirruped, 'Hi Liz, love the hair, makes you look younger.'

Then it was time for the bikini wax.

'Are you going on holiday?' the therapist from Chigwell asked me sweetly.

'No, I'm just hoping to have sex.'

FEBRUARY 20, 2000
I AM GIVEN OXYGEN

So, I'm in New York for the ready-to-wear fashion shows. I'm with the executive fashion editor of the magazine, who keeps talking about seasons, and 'sexy military' and selvedges. It's a city with no single straight men and where the women are as well-groomed as I am. Plus, it is awash with supermodels. I'm in a fancy store called Jeffrey's in the meatpacking district buying two Jil Sander T-shirts ($149 each; bargain), when who should brush past me but Gwyneth

Paltrow, all blonde hair, high heels and no make-up. It's sale time and I immediately want to rush off and tidy the shoe racks. I make my way to the Calvin Klein show to find I am seated opposite not only Gwynnie, but also Julia Roberts. My view of the two most gorgeous women in the world is interrupted every few seconds by the body of Gisele Bündchen, who bounces by in all her 19-year-old loveliness. I drag my old corpse back to my hotel, the SoHo Grand, which is full of braying young people (they already think I am mad here, because I complained about the goldfish in my room: surely, I asked the handsome male receptionist, my fish must be bored without any pondweed, and aren't round bowls disorientating?).

The next day, I take myself off to the Bliss spa on Broadway (I sound very well-travelled and sophisticated, don't I, but I'm wearing a money belt and every time I get somewhere I phone my mum to tell her I've arrived safely). I am to be renovated, much as you would a Brownstone. I start with a collagen ('Does it contain cows?') and paraffin manicure.

'So,' says the manicurist in a broad Brooklyn accent, 'ya wanna know if Gisele has any what?'

'Defects.'

'Nah, but she does have dry elbows.'

My next stop is a two-hour facial that includes deep cleansing; a fruit-acid peel that makes me very sore; an oxygen wrap; extractions, which go on for quite some time; activating massage with essential-oil balm; an ear massage (this bit is actually better than having a boyfriend); an age-fighting collagen ampoule; firming seaweed mask; arm, hand and foot massage; a hydrating hair dew treatment; and, to finish, a blast of oxygen!

The next day, I have breakfast in the lobby with my English friend Emma, who has come to live in the Village to write novels despite only being 23. She has so little fear she takes a jar of Marmite out of her bag and starts spreading it on her toast. 'So, why haven't you called him?' she asks, reminding me that I haven't spoken to The Man I Am In Love With since Millennium Eve. 'You must be a Rules girl.'

'It's not that,' I reply sadly. 'If I was a man, I wouldn't call me.'

That evening, we go to an after-show party. The bouncer stops us at the door.

'What makes you think I'm not a model?' my friend Emma asks with a remarkable amount of chutzpah.

'About six inches,' replies the bouncer.

Thank God I didn't ask that question. He probably would have said, 'About 20 years.'

Chapter 3

FEBRUARY 27, 2000
HE CALLS

He called!!! I had just got home from the Hussein Chalayan show during London Fashion Week (what can I say, the dresses turned into tables) when I found I had a message on my answerphone, saying The Man I Am In Love With really wanted to speak to me. OMIGOD!!!

I immediately phoned my best friend, Jeremy. 'What shall I do, what shall I do?' I shrieked.

'Whatever you do, don't call him back tonight. Don't act keen. Call him tomorrow.'

I called him straightaway.

'I've been meaning to call you,' he said.

'That's okay,' I said casually. 'I've been in New York and Madrid [I don't know why I said Madrid; I haven't been there since 1986]. I haven't been around much.'

'Anyway, you could have called me.'

I'm not a caller. There are three things I never do: call boys, go to shopping precincts and use public transport (it makes my hair dirty).

'I've really missed you,' he said. Hurrah! 'Do you want to see another film? Have you seen *American Beauty* yet?'

I'd been to the gala premiere. 'No, I'm dying to see it.'

We arranged to go the following Sunday, and he would call me to confirm a time. Here is where he became alarmingly blunt. 'Why did you have plastic surgery?' he asked, straight off, just like that.

'Have I?'

'On your breasts.'

My breasts: a confession

Ah. I had thought, what with the dark and the T-shirt and the vest, he might not have noticed. I did, when I was 29, have plastic surgery on my breasts, although it was not what you are thinking. I had them made smaller. I had gone through a period of not eating in my late teens to mid twenties, in a bid to stave off puberty/growing up/having to deal with boys, I don't know. Maybe I should have spent less time looking at *Vogue*. I'm not sure what triggered it but I couldn't eat. I didn't menstruate. I certainly didn't have breasts. But then I went to see my GP because I didn't have periods and he sent me to St Barts Department of Endocrinology. A professor there said I had to eat meat and have three cooked meals a day, and I was like, Yeah, like that is ever going to happen. So I would fatten myself up before an appointment with peanut-butter sandwiches and Homity pies from Cranks and weigh my coat down with plastic bottles of water to be weighed, and then I would revert to my one Loseley hazelnut yogurt and four Diet Cokes a day. So I didn't put on weight; I confounded science. The doctors then put me on steroids and my breasts grew, and I hated them, so as soon as I had enough money, I had them reduced and I now have no need to wear a bra and I love them; however, I do have scars (I don't think the surgeon sewed me up very well – he seems to have used blanket stitch) and so have always been very conscious that a potential husband might come across them and go 'Eeurgghgh!!!' and run away.

I digress. Back to the main feature
On Sunday afternoon, after a particularly strenuous week, I notice my answerphone flashing. How did I miss his call? It must have been while I was in the road, picking up crisp packets and hosing my wheelie bin. The message said that he was sorry, but he wouldn't be able to make it. He would talk to me later. Where on earth am I going wrong?

MARCH 19, 2000
HE HAS NEVER SMELT A TEDDY

I was in Tesco in my usual Saturday afternoon attire: greying T-shirt, outsize tracky bottoms, Nike slides, unwashed hair and no make-up. At weekends, I always shop in fear of bumping into anyone I remotely know, but have always assumed I am unrecognisable. I spot my ex-ex boyfriend, i.e. Mad Richard, two aisles away near the cornflakes; this is a surprise, as he never, ever went to the supermarket when he was going out with me. I thought I was going to get away with it until I was queuing with my basket (Jif, Frish, J-cloths, bleach, the Sheba gravy collection) when he parked his trolley in my rear.

'Liz?' he said, peering. I considered saying no.

'I didn't realise you still lived round here,' I said, not looking him in the eye, thinking, I was sure you'd be in prison by now.

'Yeah, my wife and I live in Highbury.'

This is the man who asked me to marry him, but never bought me a ring or called me, so I never took him that seriously.

'Why did you stop calling me?' I asked him. This wasn't the most relevant question in the world, as we had last clapped eyes on each other in 1990.

He just laughed and said, 'I knew you'd end up mad and alone and living with cats.'

I wanted to say, 'Well, who's the computer salesman?' and that I live in a house that would make John Pawson weep, but instead mumbled something about Brasso and wandered off like a homeless person.

Anyone else would have felt a bit downcast after this encounter but all I felt was relief that I hadn't married any of the men I have been involved with. Take Trevor. He had so little sense of humour that when I exclaimed with my nose in Squeaky's fur that she smelt of teddy, he said, in all seriousness, 'I've never smelt a teddy.'

The Man I Am In Love With still hasn't called. How rude.

Chapter 4

AN EXAMPLE OF WHAT WOMEN TALK ABOUT

I had dinner on Saturday night with my little friend Robi. We had just been to see *The Beach* and were discussing its merits. 'If I were a film critic,' I said, 'I wouldn't give it a good review. The sex scene was in the water, you couldn't see anything!'

What film studios have to understand is that women go to the cinema to see their favourite male movie stars in romantic comedies. We don't go to see Brad Pitt with a beard, beating someone else up; we want to see him kissing in a realistic setting.

'Okay.' I asked Robi. 'If you could sleep with any male celebrity, who would it be?'

'Ralph Fiennes,' she replied without a moment's hesitation.

'But don't you think he'd be a bit moody, like if you had a dinner party he wouldn't join in the conversation?' (My friend Beverley had a German boyfriend, a photographer called Bade, and during one dinner party he actually stood up without a word and went to bed. That is no use at all.)

'You said sleep with, not marry,' she said, sipping her organic flat rainwater from Wales. 'Anyway, what about you?'

'Prince. He is compact, meaning he wouldn't get in the way, looks very clean, is funny – that is important.'

'Well, I'm not going to introduce you to my cousin,' she said in all seriousness, 'he's got very bad posture.'

'I don't want to meet anyone else; I've already met the man I want to be with,' I said sadly. 'He's the right size, he laughs at my jokes, he appreciates the fact I know all the words to TLC's "No

Scrubs". This was our restaurant,' I said, referring to the fact we'd had our one and only meal in public here.

Robi rolled her eyes. 'Well, if I ever meet him, I'm not going to know where to look. I'm sure I'll start blushing.'

I wonder if men realise the amount of detail women go into when they talk about men. I'm sure the object of my affection hasn't even mentioned my existence to his friends (I went to Jeremy's birthday party once and was introduced to his mother and, bearing in mind that we had been best friends for about 12 years, was shocked when she said, 'And you are?'). My friends know what was said to Kevin in every phone call, how long it was (each phone call), the number of times (phone calls), etc. They know what he wears (really nice Adidas tracky bottoms), the texture of his hair, the colour of his skin and the sound he makes when he eats. I have no idea what men talk about to their friends: football, probably, and politics. I had been living with Trevor for quite some time when we went to his parents' house in Ealing to pick up some records. I was sat in the lounge on a floral settee with his slightly bewildered father.

'So,' his dad asked me politely. 'What do you do for a living?'

Chapter 5

APRIL 2, 2000

DESPITE 20 YEARS OF HIGH-IMPACT AEROBICS CLASSES, I STILL CAN'T LIFT CAT LITTER

It was just like that Macy Gray song. I lit up like a candle when he called me up. He phoned last week. We hadn't spoken since he cancelled our cinema date and we'd suddenly gone back a few stages to before we had slept together. Neither of us said anything remotely personal. But then he started emailing me, so I figured I could start to get saucy, until he told me his email was read by everyone in his office, but I thought, what the hell, and sent the following:

'Dear K. Hope you had a nice weekend. Do you fancy going to see The Hurricane with me? xx'

Having written this email, I realised my life hasn't really progressed since I was 16, except nowadays the purple Laura Ashley smock has been replaced by Jil Sander T-shirts, and the Protein 21 conditioner by Aveda Personal Blend. I still watch Saturday morning TV eating cereal and listen to the Top 40 on Sunday evening. Instead of going swimming with my friend Gail of a Saturday morning, I go to the gym (I don't understand why, after 20 years of high-impact aerobics classes, I still can't lift cat litter).

I had dinner on Saturday night with my friend India, who used to be married to Jeremy. I sat looking at all the things in her house: fridge magnets; pictures on the wall drawn by their two boys; bowls of fruit; rooms full of toys; clutter. I want that! (Well, not the clutter, obviously, or the pictures, or indeed the fridge magnets, but I would like some semblance of a life.) It's not fair. Last week, a fashion editor at the magazine was telling me all about her wedding plans. She is having a dress made by Calvin Klein, a hen night at Babington House and a honeymoon in the Maldives. She is taking scuba-diving lessons!! We had a features meeting last week, and the deputy editor, Helen, who is married to a farmer, said that we needed a single female writer to try out a new speed-dating service, and that I had to do it as I was the only person on the magazine still unattached. The shame. I'm the editor!

Chapter 6

A FEW WEEKS IN APRIL 2000, WHAT WILL BE
KNOWN AS MY HALCYON PERIOD, DURING WHICH I
MEET THE 26-YEAR-OLD

*You have to bear in mind throughout this chapter that I was, in April
2000, 36-and-a-half years old.*

One afternoon, Kerry came into my office and said she had a
young man from the BBC on the phone, who wanted to come
in and interview me for his radio station.

'Can't he do it over the phone?' I remember saying.

'No, he is quite insistent, he says he has to do it in person.'

So, a couple of days later he turned up. His name was Nirpal
Singh Dhaliwal. I remember he had short hair, was dressed head to
toe in sportswear apart from an ironed pink checked shirt, which
has never made an appearance since, and had big, shiny eyes and a
keen expression. We sat down on either side of my desk. I chatted
about the award the magazine was up for in a few days' time, and
that was it. I swear, on Squeaky's life, I thought nothing more of it.

That evening, The Man I Am In Love With phoned me. I told
him I had 'gone into a downward spiral' since the last time he called,
and he laughed. I told him he was handsome and sweet. Also bear
in mind here that he never, as far as I can recall, paid me a compliment. In fact, in flagrante on the sofa during Session Number Two,
when I asked him how old he thought I was, he had replied, 'Late
thirties, early forties?'

He said he would call me next week to go for an organic dinner,
or maybe to the curry place round the corner from where he lives.

I took great encouragement in that last bit, thinking he might, at long last, INVITE ME BACK FOR COFFEE.

I think feng shui might actually work. I had kept Kevin's photograph under my pillow all week, and then he calls! I forgot to move it on the day my cleaner, H, came; when I got home she had propped it on the mantelpiece. Aside from the fact she has to use a new J-cloth every time she cleans the bathroom and then 'throw it away!' (I demonstrated the action of throwing it away much as Basil would to Manuel), she must now well and truly believe that I am bonkers. I am sure she doesn't really want me to get a boyfriend, as that would mean more mess, and stains.

Anyway, back to The 26-year-old. I had gone to the awards ceremony with Kerry, and spotted him across the room. I suppose I stared for quite some time, but this was in the days before I had laser eye surgery. 'It's Nirpal,' I whispered to Kerry, and we both smiled and he came over. That is all that happened.

The next day, I got an email from him. 'Kerry, come and read this,' I said.

It read: 'Nice to see you again the other day. I am thinking of setting up a web site, and wanted to pick your brains. Could I take you out to dinner? N x'

'But that's great!' piped Kerry, pointing to the 'x'. 'Just marry anyone soon and you could be in *Hello!*'

'He can't possibly fancy me,' I said. 'Anyway, I'm already going out with someone.' She looked doubtful.

'Well,' she continued, 'he didn't touch me on the arm and ask for my email address.'

I typed back: 'I don't know anything about web sites and I am really, really busy.'

His reply popped back: 'Neither do I. I'm sure we'll have plenty of other things to talk about.'

I thought that was rather forward, but it made a change from Kevin, so I emailed: 'Okay, Friday night, at Rasa in Stoke Newington.'

'Great,' came his reply. 'I'm vegetarian, too. My treat.'

APRIL 22–23, 2000
THE ONE GLORIOUS WEEKEND IN
WHICH I DOUBLE-PARKED

Well, finally, on the Friday evening I was supposed to be seeing The 26-year-old (I emailed to cancel, but he re-scheduled for the Saturday, and Actually Phoned the Restaurant to Re-Book), I went out for dinner with The Man I Am In Love With, at the cheap curry house near his flat. He was late. Despite the fact I was all in cream – buttery suede Alberta Ferretti trousers, cream suede Calvin Klein bag, cream desert boots, tawny highlights – he didn't pass comment on my appearance. Perhaps he is blind.

He told me about a couple of bands he had seen play at the Jazz Cafe. I asked him if he wanted to go with me to see Joaquín Cortés at Sadler's Wells, and he said, 'No, it's not really my sound.' When it came to the bill, which was £13.50, he said, 'Sorry I can only get my half.' We got in the Beetle and drove back to my place, where we had sex, once, with Squeaky on the bed being jiggled up and down (I considered blindfolding her). I remember noticing my light bulb needed dusting. He left at 2 a.m.

All in all, can you blame me for going out with The 26-year-old the following evening? He had already left several messages on my mobile, checking that I was actually going to turn up, so I didn't have the heart to cancel. I got to the restaurant, and he was already there, all upright and alert. I ordered a glass of wine. I told him I had a boyfriend. He told me he still lived with his mum in Greenford, and that, being Easter Saturday, it had taken him two and a half hours to get to the restaurant by public transport. I felt so guilty that at the end of the meal, which he paid for, I offered him a lift home (which was annoying, as I had expressly chosen that restaurant to save me driving far, and so that I would get home in time for *Frasier*; he, years later, told me that he thought I had chosen it so that I could take him back to my place – the cheek!).

Anyway, on the Marylebone flyover, he squeezed my knee. He will later deny this, but he did, definitely. Perhaps it was due to fear; I tend to drive like Mrs Magoo. We stopped in his road, outside his house. He invited me in, but I was scared of meeting his mum in case she was younger than me. He went to kiss me goodbye, and it turned into a snog. He put his hand down my Pocahontas trousers and I remember thinking: Don't stretch them! He will swear to this day I did something rather rude to him in the front seat, and that I pounced on him. Well, perhaps I did. All I can say is that he wasn't wearing pants. I was feeling confident; I'd had some practice the night before.

We drove all the way back to my house at top speed. He was immediately divested of his trainers: he got his hopes up at this point, but was soon disappointed when I told him I don't allow shoes in the house, only paws, and that I was also slightly worried by his socks. I introduced him to Snoopy and Squeaky ('Why,' I could see him thinking, 'if she's such a fuss pot, is the fat black one allowed to sit on the bread board?'), and he actually bent down to their height to introduce himself, which I thought was a good sign. We had sex on the sofa, quite a remarkable feat for me as I HATE anything riling it up; I don't even sit on it to eat spaghetti with tomato sauce. We went to bed. I have to say he was a very good lover, not that I had much to compare him with (merely steamy passages in Julie Myserson novels and a well-worn tape of *Dirty Dancing*). His kisses were firm and urgent. He liked to pull my hair. I became quite sore. He sweated a lot. He had a sweet little round tummy and hairy footballer's legs.

The next day, being Easter Sunday, meant I had to go and visit my mum in Saffron Walden.

'Won't your mum be wondering where you are?' I asked him, worried he hadn't been able to clean his teeth.

'No, I told her I wouldn't be coming back last night,' he smirked.

'How did you know I was going to let you stay the night?' I asked.

'You had it written all over you at the awards ceremony,' he said. 'I could tell by the way you kept staring that you really fancied me.'

I dropped him off at Holborn station. That, I thought, trying to get into second gear, is the last I will ever see of him.

Chapter 7

MAY 7, 2000
I HAVE LOTS OF EMAIL

So, The 26-year-old asked me to the cinema. He had sent me an email, which I inadvertently let Kerry read over my shoulder. It read: 'You still sore? Shall I kiss it better?'

'Sauce!' Kerry shouted.

I told him I wanted to see *Being John Malkovich*. He paid for the cinema tickets, which I thought was sweet as he probably still has a student loan. Our age difference (of which MUCH MORE later) rather than being a source of conflict became, during the course of our second weekend together, a source of amusement, at least on his part. When he brought me up a cup of coffee and a biscuit in bed, he said it was like I was, and I quote, his 'Nan'. All the next day he kept telling me I should watch my step, in case I fell and broke my hip.

'Well, if you are going to play dirty,' I countered, eyeing his outsize jeans with the crotch halfway to his knees, 'which one are you, Kriss or Kross?'

He did, though, pay me lots of compliments, which made a refreshing change. He said I was in 'good nick', had a 'lovely tummy', which he had spotted in my office, and that my hands were my Unique Selling Point. However, the Nan analogies re-emerged when he discovered I am as blind as a bat and that both my cats sleep on my bed, with their own pillows.

The next weekend was also spent with The 26-year-old, from 9.15 p.m. on Friday until after midnight on Sunday. We only ventured out once, on Saturday afternoon. The rest of the time was spent ordering vegetarian takeaways and ordering films on Sky Box Office and me trying to put his socks in the washing machine. He saw me without make-up and didn't run away screaming. We even talked about what our child would be like ('It would have my hair and eyelashes,' he said, 'and your teeth and hands.') He later told me his best female friend, Bunmi, told him off for missing her barbecue.

Young men, I discovered, not having known any intimately when I was of the same vintage, are very insecure. 'You haven't given me one compliment all weekend,' he moaned, 'and I've given you loads.'

'Yes I have,' I said, trying to remember. 'I said your feet are like paddles so you must be able to swim well.'

During the week, I emailed him. 'Have you gone off me? My elbows are sore. x'

His reply read: 'A little bit.... (COURSE NOT!) Want to do something this weekend, an exhibition maybe? What did I do to your elbows? xx'

Now, I don't like exhibitions or walking round looking at things, usually because my shoes hurt, so I suggested he come to my house on Saturday night. He phoned late on Friday.

'Hi,' he said, and I could tell he was lying on his mattress. 'I've really missed you. I've been playing the tape of when I interviewed you just to hear your voice [!]. I had a great time last weekend.'

'I wasn't sure what it meant,' I said.

'What do you mean? It was getting to know each other, it was really cool. No pressure.'

'No,' I said. 'In the film, how did all those people go in to John Malkovich's head?'

He laughed. 'You know, I've been thinking,' he murmured, 'about me not wanting to be your boyfriend [didn't he? why not?]. Because I do. It might not be for ever, but we can see how it goes. I don't want to add more stress to your life, always wondering if I'm with another woman.'

I had thought he would probably be playing football in the street, but still.

'Because on Wednesday night,' he continued, 'I slept with some-one else.'

Chapter 8

NUMBER OF OCCASIONS ON WHICH MEN
HAVE DISAPPOINTED ME

1. When I first came up to London as a student, a man in Tottenham Court Road asked me out for a drink. I duly met him in a pub, and he asked me what I wanted to drink. 'Diet Coke,' I replied. He went up to the bar, and seemed to be gone for rather a long time. I waited about an hour. He never came back.

2. Kevin Griffin (what is it with all these Kevins?). It was 1989, and The Sunday Times Christmas party at the ICA on the Mall. Kevin was a photographer, and because he cycled everywhere he wore brightly coloured spandex. He had long, blond hair. He started chatting to me (I noticed he was dribbling beer down his front), and suggested we leave together. We went for a curry. Walking me to the bus stop, he told me had a girlfriend, and then, in Trafalgar Square, near the National Portrait Gallery, we kissed. He felt very damp. He wanted to come home with me but I refused, thinking my legs hadn't been waxed. That weekend I went to Boots and bought K-Y jelly, remembering the skiing fiasco. I bumped into him from time to time at work but HE NEVER SPOKE TO ME AGAIN.

3. Trevor. He could be nominated for many different occasions, but I have to say that one of them was the moment he told me he was seeing Jenny the stylist (not Jenni with the concrete) while I was trying to negotiate Hyde Park Corner. Another was when after SIX YEARS he phoned me at my office at the magazine, not to ask me how I was, or whether I seeing anyone, or to say sorry my dad had died, or did I still have the Beetle, but to ask me if I knew how to get hold of any cheap flights to Jamaica.

4. Kevin. For not phoning me often enough. For not paying for dinner, even though it was only £13.50. For leaving it until it was FAR TOO LATE to declare his intentions.

5. David Scrace, for not marrying me or even asking me out. For going out with Wilma.

6. My husband, for saying age doesn't matter and that he will always love me, when it does, and he won't.

Chapter 9

MAY 21, 2000
HE BEGS ME NOT TO SEE KEVIN AGAIN

Well, I forgave The 26-year-old. I don't think, at this point, that I was in love with him. And I was the one who had, remember, spectacularly double-parked. I took him to a party given by Ricky Martin at the Armani shop in Knightsbridge. I introduced him to lots of my friends and colleagues, and to Jeremy (who had been privy to large amounts of detail and did well not to splutter into his Sea Breeze). At 11.30 p.m. I told him I wanted to leave. And later, I'm afraid we had our first argument, in bed.

'I kept trying to give you a hug and kiss you hello, and you kept pushing me away,' he moaned. 'And as soon as I got there you wanted to leave.'

'Yes, well, I hate couples,' I replied. 'And I introduced you to everyone.'

'Yeah, I think you liked showing off your little Asian boy, but you wanted to keep me at arm's length.'

'I'm not used to going to a party with a man,' I said. Which is true. All my life I have gone out – to discos, to awful parties with boxes of cider and sticky floors, to really noisy clubs in west London, to bars with my friends Donna and India – with the express purpose of trying to meet someone. I was hopeless at college. I had a crush on the law lecturer, Charles (he was a dead ringer for Paul Nicholas), and spent ages looking out of the refectory trying to spot his car (a cream Beetle). The only time he ever spoke to me I was in a pub, post a performance of *The Match Girls* (don't ask) with my stage make-up still on, all lights and shadows and wrinkles (I was playing the ancient Mrs P; I realise now that stood for Pankhurst, but at the time the plot went over my head) and needless to say he never spoke to me again.

The next morning, after the argument, I woke up to a really friendly, flirty phone message from The Man I Am In Love With, confirming we would be seeing each other that evening. The 26-year-old overheard it (these really were Halcyon days), and went off in a strop for a bath. I told him off for splashing. We went out for lunch and he refused to talk to me. I told him I would drop him off at the underground station, as I had to get ready for my date. This may sound harsh, but he is the one who slept with someone else, remember; he said in his defence that he hadn't really fancied her, but felt he was 'on a roll' and should capitalise on it. We sat in my car outside Old Street.

'Don't see him, blow him out,' he pleaded.

'But you are too young for me, you'll just end up running off with a younger woman.'

'Men your age will run off with younger women,' he argued.

I drove home, and got ready in record time. I went to pick up Kevin, and when he emerged from his flat, in orange track pants, his hair bouncing, I fell in love with him all over again.

'So, Miss Jones,' he said, kissing me on the cheek. 'What have you been up to this weekend?'

MONDAY MORNING

I'm sitting at my desk at work, reading the papers, but I can't concentrate. Last night, Kevin did that thing where we regressed a few stages, like I was a work colleague or an ancient aunt, when on parking my car outside his flat he kissed me on both cheeks and darted inside as fast as his dodgy knee could carry him. What is wrong with him? I thought men would have sex whenever the opportunity arose; they hire prostitutes, for goodness' sake. To be honest, my abortive dates with Kevin are not good for my already fragile ego. I have had enough of people like him and David Scrace. I am nice. I am clean. Maybe I should give The 26-year-old more of a chance. But he is so terribly young, almost new born. He doesn't remember Magpie, or the Bay City Rollers, or the day Diana married Charles. He would have been too small for a Chopper bike. He doesn't know what a feather cut is; if he had gone to Live Aid, he would have had to sit on someone's shoulders in order to see anything. But he is so keen. It makes such a nice change from being ignored. It will all end in tears. But maybe it won't. I'm pretty well preserved. I've done everything the glossies told me to do: moisturised and exfoliated and limited facial expressions. I could pass muster as someone who isn't his mum. I could, couldn't I?

Fear of ageing

I haven't always been cagey about how old I am. This has only been the case in the last ten years or so. The 26-year-old might have been joking when he went on (and on) about propping me up on pillows, asking if I would like a Rich Tea, and if I still possessed a tank top, but I knew then that it would, one day, although not quite as quickly as it actually did, turn out to be an insurmountable problem. He could learn to be tidier, to find out how to switch the central heating on, where the stop cock is, what Brasso is for and so forth, but I could never, ever be younger. Why did it take so long to find someone who liked me back? When I found David Scrace, I was actually eight years younger than he was.

For one thing, it is very tiring keeping up with the vagaries of youth culture. Okay, so I know that J-Lo is a person, not a toilet cleaner, but I find it impossible to tell Ant from Dec. I have no desire to see *Shrek*. We couldn't watch any of those 'I Love 1973' TV programmes together – at least not until they reached the late eighties. And when we go out I like to eat in nice restaurants with tablecloths and a wine list. Waiters often ask The 26-year-old if he wants an orange squash.

Anyone would think I am ageing faster than other people, like those two women in a particular episode of *Star Trek* who turn in to old crones while Captain Kirk is kissing them. Contrary to what my friend Jeremy thinks, I am NOT older than Michael Jackson or Madonna, but having such a youthful admirer is a constant reminder to use anti-ageing masks and to sleep with my hands covered in gunk inside special gloves and my feet in Bliss Soothing Foot Salve inside a pair of Bliss Softening Socks.

If I were a professional footballer, my career would most definitely be over by now. I can still, in theory, have children, but I am definitely beginning to show my age. I now, having become addicted to BBC2's rather excellent gardening programmes, know the names of plants other than geraniums. When The 26-year-old uses the word 'Safe', there are a few moments before I realise he does not mean he remembered to turn off the gas and turn on the burglar alarm. Our age difference doesn't cause too many problems at the moment apart from the fact he doesn't know who Shep was, or how difficult it was when he died. Still, at least I hope we'll die at roughly the same time.

But it's exhausting, just keeping on top of my grey roots, the constant moisturising, the spin classes, the swimming, the listening to endless hours of Radio 1. I nearly died when I found out his mum has only just turned fifty. I worry about my elbows, about my upper arms, about crepey skin, about reading glasses, about the fact I now prefer *A Place in the Sun* to *The OC*. What is wrong with me? I have to say that at this point in our relationship, The 26-year-old actually thought I was three and a half years younger than I was (I didn't tell him my real age until two weeks before we got married; he consequently pranged the car). Perhaps that is why I then started to be quite mean to him. I wanted him to go away and leave me alone, not see me descend into a whiskery husk.

Chapter 10

MAY 28, 2000

I AM MEAN TO HIM AS
A SELF-PRESERVATION TACTIC

He is beginning to get on my nerves. I sent him off to buy sugar, milk and tea bags and he was gone for hours. I resigned myself to the fact that he had simply sloped off home, and had an oily bath. I was surprised when he tapped on the front door.

'Where have you been?' I squeaked.

'Well, I wanted to buy you some grapes, so I had to walk miles until I found a greengrocer,' he said, exhausted (living in Hackney, the only produce you can buy are sweets, alcohol and drugs). He then made my muesli, but he had bought ordinary milk, not organic, so I told him off.

'You've ruined my breakfast!' I wailed like a baby.

'I can never do anything right,' he said miserably. 'When I brought flowers to the restaurant I could see you didn't like them.' (I am very fussy about flowers; I don't like dark green leaves, or anything spiky.)

I have been behaving, it has to be said, like a complete cow. I tell him off for wearing jeans on the sofa, for leaving the scratchy pad in the sink, for not knowing how to turn the central heating on, for not having a credit card or a wallet, for splashing, for making crumbs. And he takes it all, without a murmur, merely telling me how much he loves me. But I can't fall in love with him, I can't. I want Kevin, The Man I Am In Love With. I don't want a boy. We'll never be able to go on holiday together in case he sees my passport. I can never take him to meet my mum in case she gets out old black-

and-white photos of me. I wasn't even young enough to enjoy punk properly. Nothing will come of this. I am wasting my time.

Chapter 11

JUNE 4, 2000
WE GO ON HOLIDAY TO
JAMAICA AND FALL IN LOVE

I have just got off the phone to Kevin. I asked him to go away with me to Jamaica to stay at Goldeneye, where Ian Fleming wrote James Bond, and he turned me down. Flat. He said he was far too busy. Tempted, but far too busy. I have to be honest: it was a blow.

I then asked The 26-year-old. I came clean, and said he wasn't my first choice. He was so annoyed he also turned me down. We went to see *Mission Impossible 2* on Friday night. 'Do you like my new trainers?' he asked, in all seriousness.

'Do they light up as you walk?' I enquired meanly.

'Yeah, my mum bought them for me so that I don't get run over,' he replied good-naturedly. He asked me if I had any food in the house.

'Umm, I think I've got a banana,' I said.

I don't know why he is still going out with me. So I asked him.

'Well, I don't know either,' he said. 'You never phone me, you never have any milk and you're seeing someone else. Plus, you're really difficult.'

'I'm not difficult, I'm easy going!' I said indignantly.

'You're hard work: you tell me not to drip anywhere; when we're in bed I always end up on the edge; and you're always getting up in the middle of the night to follow your cats around.'

'That's normal,' I protested.

I asked Jeremy if he thought I was difficult. 'Yes, you're bonkers,' he said disloyally. 'When you meet someone new, you never understand what they say and stare at them blankly. You always show if you're bored and you're always telling waiters what you don't like on the menu: pesto, fennel, peppers, onions, things with bits, mushrooms, rocket, anything eggy.'

Charming. Well, I am going to get in some provisions as soon as the kitchen is finished. I'm having a limestone floor; industrial steel appliances; an open fire; lights from Sweden; Nicole Farhi wonky china; ingredients like sea salt and balsamic vinegar. Even saucepans. I might even get a whisk so that I can bake Victoria sponges.

Anyway, The 26-year-old did come with me to Jamaica. He told me later he had consulted his best friend David, who told him he might as well go for a free holiday as he could always dump me when he got back. On the flight, he watched *Austin Powers: The Spy Who Shagged Me* and found the scene in the tent particularly funny. After the two-hour taxi ride we arrived at our little house overlooking the bay. We tiptoed down the steps to the beach and paddled, gazing up at the millions of stars, and then slept beneath a mosquito net with a fan gently whirring over our heads. The room had a giant bath in it (in which we had sex; I remember his erection popped out of the bubbles, like a periscope), and an outdoor shower. Tiny frogs tiddly-winked across the stone floor.

I remember the moment I fell in love with him. He had sheepishly fished a wad of paper out of his rucksack for me to read on the beach. It was the first couple of chapters of his book. He then went and stood waist deep in the water while I read it. It was really good: dark and funny and honest and rude. He, by then quite wrinkled, waded back to shore, which was really difficult because he was wearing combat shorts, and his pockets had filled with sand and water.

'My God,' I told him. 'It's good. Have you really visited a prostitute and snogged a man?' (He admitted he had, on both counts.) 'You should write it; you should give up your day job and write your novel. It's too good not to.'

'You really think so?' he asked, all chuffed.

Chapter 12

HOW I ALSO FELL IN LOVE WITH FOOTBALL

The 26-year-old (who I think from hereon in can be referred to as The Boyfriend) is a football lunatic, a Spurs fan ('Glen has come home!' was the gist of a four-hour telephone conversation with David) whose knowledge of Europe is marked out by football stadia, whose command of foreign languages consists of words like Bundesliga and Primera Liga, whose uncanny total recall of every score line predates the year of his birth (1974, the year Germany beat Holland 2–1 to win the World Cup, the irrepressible Gerd Muller scoring the winner), but who can never remember a list of more than three items to buy in Tesco Express.

I have to say, football spoilt our lovely holiday in Jamaica. Despite the perfect weather and starlit nights, our own private beach and humming-bird-filled garden, we sat inside, curtains drawn, to watch every single match of Euro 2000. Our flight home was brought forward to ensure we were in time for the final. Whenever we have been on holiday since, we have had to check out the dimensions of the TV; the availability of satellite; the time difference. When we went to Italy in May 2000, and were admiring the view from our terrace overlooking the red roofs of Florence, instead of pointing out the Duomo he excitedly directed my gaze to the hallowed turf of Fiorentina (perennial under achievers despite having had some of the game's greatest players, notably Baggio, Costa, Battistuta et al; it will be interesting to see how the new manager, Roberto Mancini, fares this season).

Like many football widows, my knowledge of the sport pre-football-obsessed boyfriend consisted of knowing the names of Ryan Giggs and Stan Collymore, and occasionally watching an FA Cup Final. I had watched, I told The Boyfriend proudly soon after we met, the England versus Argentina game in the last World Cup when David Beckham was sent off ('so unfair, his poor crumpled face!'). I couldn't remember the final score, though. When asked the name of my favourite player I would nominate Michael Owen because of his little arms and schoolboy haircut. I thought the 2001/2 season would involve Kate Moss and Dries Van Noten. I thought a player cam was something they carried around, that the fans changed ends at half time, that the players wore a uniform, and that if a game was drawn it could always go into overtime. I didn't think much of goalies; I thought they just stood there, bored, drinking from a flask and listening to the radio.

My aversion to football began in the seventies, the heyday of the game according to the experts (the decade of Pele, Cruyff and Best), but it was the bane of my childhood, especially with three older brothers and showjumping on the other side. Football in those days was also very muddy, and the players weren't nearly as glamorous as they are today, although Charlie George was something of a heart-throb in Form 3B. Players such as Malcolm MacDonald and Nobby Stiles had no teeth or hair but they still wore impossibly tight shorts. Chris Waddle had a mullet. They were also far less fit, seeming rather puny compared with the six-packed Adonises of today, who emerge from the showers wearing designer suits, a crisp shirt and a healthy glow.

Until recently, my most vivid football memory was watching the Everton captain (waiting intently in the Wembley tunnel before the FA Cup final) scratch his testicles and play with his foreskin prior to shaking hands with the Queen. I didn't even know that European matches were televised until last year. I would occasionally tune in to *Match of the Day* just for Gary Lineker, who I thought was very kind to Paul Gascoigne during the Italia 1990 World Cup, and for Alan Hansen, who has, unlike most football players, aged very well.

But as I began to watch football with The Boyfriend, I began to yearn less for *Dawson's Creek* and to actually pay attention. For the first few months I tended to get on his nerves. I would ask several times which way the players were going. I would object to various players being substituted and less attractive ones brought on (when asked by The Boyfriend what my objection to Paul Scholes was, I replied he had a good body but that 'I wouldn't go out with that head'). Martin Keown should not be playing at all. A little knowledge proved to be a dangerous thing: we were watching a friendly between France and Portugal when I exclaimed that Man United's latest signing was playing for France. 'No he's not,' The Boyfriend corrected me, 'he can't play for France.'

'Why not?' I wailed.

'Because he's Dutch.'

But after several months of intensive tutoring, during which I sat through every match the TV could churn out, including the Second Division playoffs and the Copa America (which seemed to last all summer), I can now appreciate the finer aspects of the game – though not the offside rule, goal difference and games played in two legs. I can even appreciate that managers have the worst job – it's a bit like being the editor of a glossy magazine: one bad result and you're out.

For women new to the game I recommend the Spanish and Italian leagues wholeheartedly: the players have long black hair, olive skin, vicious tempers and enormous thighs. There was a great moment before the end of Roma versus Parma when the fans ran excitedly onto the pitch (Roma being minutes away from winning their first championship in 17 years) and stripped the players down to their pants. I now know the names of all the greats: Rivaldo (the skinny one); Figo (the very expensive one who looks like Action Man); Zinedine Zidane (the balding, Zen-like one). It really isn't that difficult, although at the start of the new season they all seem to be playing for different teams, showing no loyalty at all. My favourite at the moment is the veteran Italian defender Paolo Maldini, who has played for AC Milan since he was a boy and has light eyes and dark skin. Mmmm.

Chapter 13

So we get back from Jamaica just in time to watch the Euro 2000 final in which France cheat and beat Italy. We had had a bit of an argument on the plane home, when I had asked him to move in with me to write his novel, and he had said he wasn't sure.

'Why not? Why?' I whined. I am now definitely in love with him, but I so wish I wasn't.

'I've been meaning to tell you all week,' he said. 'The night before we left, I went to Soho with David and I met this girl and took her number.' (This argument will from this point forward be known as, 'the first time you dumped me'.) 'But I threw her number away!' he pleaded. 'I was just flirting.'

'But you had your rucksack with you,' I said incongruously.

'I know. I told her I was going to Jamaica the next day with a friend.'

Now, if there is one thing that makes me angry, other than eating standing up without a plate, it is when a man I have been sharing my innermost thoughts with, who has seen me without my top on, denies that I am, in fact, his girlfriend. Men have said to me over the years: 'I love you but I'm not in love with you' (that was Trevor); 'I'm not ready for a relationship' (Mad Richard); and 'Did we ever go out, really?' (that was Kevin, quite recently, and he did have a point).

I got my own back when I replayed my phone messages, and there was one from Kevin, The Man I Was In Love With. The Boyfriend hovered in the background (if he had hoovered in the background, that would have been more useful).

'Who did you tell him you were going to Jamaica with?' he asked me.

'I told him I was going on my own,' I said, deliberately not pressing erase. I can always throw the number away later.

JULY 16, 2000
HE MOVES IN

He is now living with me. It didn't happen after a great discussion, merely that after we got back from Jamaica he failed to ever go home again. He would trot off to work in the morning in brightly coloured beachwear, cut-off trousers and giant flip-flops. But, after just one week, I'm afraid we have come to blows. On Friday morning, in a taxi on the way to work, I told him off for spilling coffee in bed and for leaving a wet towel on the pillow. Later on that day, he sent me the following email:

'Lizzie. Having contemplated this morning, and in discussion with my mate Caroline... We concur that coffee on the bed isn't a serious crime (coffee gets spilt... c'est la vie); leaving a wet towel on the bed is wholly avoidable and worthy of reprimand... but did u need to ball me out in front of the cabbie? It was embarrassing and hurtful. Annihilating me in public is quite your forte. Remember, I have options...' he concluded ominously.

That weekend, I had to leave him alone in the house because I was going to Paris for the couture collections. 'The only things you have to remember are, not to wear shoes in the house, and that the cats, from hereon in known as your step-pets, are your Number One Priority.'

'Where's the cat food?' he mumbled, a little cavalierly I thought.

'They only eat human food,' I explained, as if to a child. 'Cat food contains euthanised former once-loved pets. They are allowed human tuna. Human chicken. Snoop likes pasta.'

In Paris, I was really homesick. 'How are the step-pets?' I asked him, trying to keep the hysteria out of my voice.

'Squeak licked me until I gave her my cornflakes,' he murmured sleepily. 'Snoop's cool. I'm afraid I didn't get the washing in cos it was raining.'

'Thank you for the poems,' I said. He had stashed some in my suitcase – his favourite Ted Hughes one and a few lines from the Bhagvadgita. 'And the flowers.'

'I didn't send you flowers.' Oh. They must be from a fashion PR. (Sometimes when I go to the shows, my room looks as though someone has died. Fashion people love sending flowers; mention a designer's name in a caption and you will receive 60 identical tulips. Funny, when I left the magazine a few months later, I didn't get so much as a daffodil.)

'I've been smelling your clothes,' he said dreamily. 'I'll cook you dinner when you get home. I love you!'

I love you too, darling. I really, really do.

JULY 23, 2000
THE MAN I WAS IN LOVE WITH CALLS
AT AN INOPPORTUNE MOMENT

We gave our first dinner party as a couple on Friday night. We had spinach tart ('It's like you,' The Boyfriend said when I brought it home from Clarke's. 'A large vegetarian tart') and lamb's lettuce and new potatoes and strawberries and Hill Station ice cream and Illy coffee. The evening went as planned, except Squeak gave Little Friend Robi asthma, and then she attacked Kerry's boyfriend (Squeak, not Robina). But the worst moment, the incident that put a real dampener on it, was when The Man I Was In Love With called at about 11.30 p.m. The Boyfriend had picked up the phone, and handed it to me, stony faced. I took it upstairs and stood chatting by the window.

'I've really missed you,' he cooed. 'I've just been mugged outside my front door, can you come over?'

'Umm,' I said, and turned round to see The Boyfriend stood in the doorway, his mouth a wiggly line, like Charlie Brown's. 'It's a bit awkward…'

'When are you going to come and see my new flat?' he said. 'I wish I'd gone to Jamaica with you.' Oh God. Why do men ignore you for months and the minute you give a dinner party they get all keen? And with that, I said goodbye and put the phone down.

The next day, we drove to The Boyfriend's house to pick up the rest of his things. He actually had posters in his room, and long-abandoned mugs. He started putting clothes in a bin bag and then proceeded to line up 15 pairs of trainers. 'Do you really need all those?' I squeaked, suddenly wishing I had a garage. He then started heaving piles of house music CDs on to my back seat. I have given him 24 hours to unpack all his stuff; otherwise it will all just fester in the hallway. I tell him the house now smells of boy. Why do men never notice anything, by the way? Such as, that the washing machine has finished its cycle (mine actually tells you when it has finished). Why do they never put CDs back in the correct cases? Why do they leave piles of coins everywhere? What is with the weird scraps of paper on the mantelpiece?

'I saw how untidy your bedroom was,' I told him. 'I've spent four years getting my house just the way I want it.'

'Don't be such an old biddy,' he said, giving me a bear hug. I suppose I am lucky that he is so laid back, that he didn't mind when his trainers got soaked while I was giving them an airing.

'You're not going to leave me for that woolly-haired chump, are you?' he asked. 'Not when I've just moved in all my stuff?'

AUGUST 6, 2000
I WORRY ABOUT MY HOUSE

The girls in the office are comparing notes about the worst thing their boyfriends have ever done. The boyfriend who won had let his girlfriend's parents' dogs out the back door, and they had been run over on the motorway. Killing pets is much worse than being smelly or untidy or having an affair.

I am in New York, and have left my two cats in the care of The Boyfriend. As I set off, I handed him two A4 sheets of instructions, which included the obvious points, such as to put their bowls in the dishwasher and to cut the chicken into bite-size pieces, as well as the less obvious but equally important ones, such as to dispose of dental floss sensibly, to be careful when opening and closing the chest of drawers, and that Squeaky likes to eat on the kitchen windowsill so that she can look out at the garden.

I would imagine that the worst thing for any boyfriend is to be left alone in the girlfriend's house. He wouldn't have time for anything raucous, he would be too busy pulling up dandelions, mowing the lawn ('Mind Squeaky!!'), plumping up the sofa cushions and taping *Dawson's Creek*.

Living with a man, I have discovered that they aren't really multi-skilled. If I ask him a question while he is emptying the dishwasher, he doesn't reply. He doesn't remember which towel is his or that it might occasionally need washing ('Why?' he whined. 'Because it is full of old water,' I said).

I am in New York with the very loyal Kerry shooting a cover. It worries me that The Boyfriend might:

1. Start a fire. He also has a very cavalier attitude towards leaving tea towels around.

2. Lose one of the cats, or sit on Squeaky.

3. Answer the phone to Kevin.

'Have you ever had an affair?' Kerry asked me. I said that I had tried once. When Trevor had gone to his mum's, I had invited Mad Richard round for dinner, but I couldn't go through with the actual sex part. Anyway, why would I cheat on someone who tells me twenty times a day he loves me, has become a vegetarian and lets Snoop stand on his chest; who sleeps like a long-dead starfish so that he doesn't disturb the cats; who calls Squeaky 'darling'? I am beginning to regret being so mean to him. The other day, I asked him why he doesn't drive, and told him that he is pathetic and useless. 'What if we went to Wales for the weekend?' I asked him.

'I'd navigate, and pass you boiled sweets.'

What more could I want in a man?

AUGUST 20, 2000
TEETHING PROBLEMS

My little friend Robi phoned last night to tell me about her weekend with her new boyfriend, Deep. She informs me she is still at the skin-brushing and exfoliating stage, which made me hanker for the days when I was frantically honing. I asked The Boyfriend if he minded, now that we are living together, that I am not always lounging around in Tse cashmere pants and a Prada cami, lit seductively by Diptyque candles, but instead wear men's Gap PJs and a huge grey sweatshirt (his, he has just realised). He said he hadn't really noticed the difference.

'Do you mean that when we used to go on dates, you never noticed the effort I had gone to, the body polishing and the eyelash separating with a pin?' I asked him, aghast.

'No, but I always thought you looked really clean.'

Why do men always manage to say the wrong thing? When he picked me up recently to drop me on the bed, I asked him how much he thought I weighed. 'Oooh, about 11 stone?' he said cautiously.

Anyway, he is having second thoughts about having moved in and is thinking of going back to his mum's, although she has already converted his bedroom into an office. He says my extreme tidiness and tea-towel ironing makes the acid rise in his stomach.

'I'm not as bad as all that, am I? I said you don't have to make the bed if Snoopy is still on it.'

He proceeded to recite a long list of my favourite sayings:

'Mind Squeaky!'

'The washing machine is not a work surface.'

'I want to watch *Frasier*.'

'Ow!' (He is very clumsy, and is always trapping my hair.)

AUGUST 27, 2000
WE GO ON OUR FIRST MINI BREAK, AND FIND IT IS
THE AUGMENTER OF DOOM

I tried to set up my feisty friend Jenni (of the concrete) on a blind date last week. I invited her along for a drink to meet The Boyfriend and his best friend, David. Now, David is handsome and intelligent, and remarkably well built, having just spent a year training to be a boxer for a book. It is the first time I have ever seen Jenni lost for words. 'You don't fancy David more than me, do you?' The Boyfriend asked when we got home.

Truth be known, women don't like men to be too handsome. I like a man to be chubby, so that I seem thin by comparison. When I lived with Trevor, he would make me cut his hair (he was on some sort of economy drive) and I secretly made him look bald at the back to discourage other women. I have started feeding Pringles to The Boyfriend. He said the other day that he is the most hen-pecked person he knows. 'Who else,' he moaned, 'is left a note asking him to clear out the little tray under the toaster. Who?'

We decided to go on a mini break, to stay with my Italian girl-friend Allegra, or Leggy. We had a slight incident at Stansted Airport when he knocked coffee over me, and I told him to 'f*** off'. He later told me he almost dumped me there and then. I can say with all honesty I have never sworn at him since September 5, 2000, forever remembered as The Day You Dumped Me On My Birthday.

We spent Saturday on the beach, and I was amazed at the beauty of the women, who wore hot-pink sarongs that they would check in the full-length mirrors. They had clearly never heard of the term 'Factor 15'.

The Boyfriend spent the entire time eyeing up perfect, round buttocks, flat tummies and upper arms taut from toting Louis Vuitton beach bags. Italian teenagers are so much more beautiful than British ones: dark little limbs like sticks, pale eyes and tawny hair, leaning on Vespas and sipping coffee. I spent my teenage years in a Laura Ashley mauve smock huddled in a windswept bus shelter.

I have a question here. Leggy gave a dinner party for twenty in her garden, and The Boyfriend had two plates of pasta, a vat of red wine and two helpings of cake – he'd already had two custard croissants that morning. But he didn't look any different. After two plates of pasta, I looked as if I was about to give birth to a small hippo. How does that work? Why do only women change shape after food? We went to bed in the small cabin in the grounds, and he demanded his nuptials. I said that I can't have sex after food. 'No, no, you're confusing sex with swimming,' he said, crestfallen.

We get back home, and the next morning, I find he has locked Snoopy by mistake in the broom cupboard. He was traumatised (Snoopy). The Boyfriend tried to apologise, and picked him up.

'Don't pick him up!' I yelled. 'It abuses his civil rights.'

We always have our arguments in the morning, so he has been barred from getting out of bed until I have gone to work.

But it seems no matter how much I tell him off (*see above*, in which I am mean to him as a self-preservation tactic), he adores me unconditionally. He leaves notes for me to find all over the house, saying if I ever leave him for a Hollywood hot shot, he is going to fight me for custody of his step-pets. (He is referring to the dinner party in Tuscany, when I was chatted up by a twat called Simon and The Boyfriend sat between us, getting more and more annoyed at both of us as we brayed 'Yes, Jennifer Aniston is SO LOVELY!', until he blurted out that he got four As in his A-levels.)

He is under enormous pressure at the moment, because it is my birthday on Tuesday. He knows what a nightmare I am to buy presents for. If he buys me flowers, they have to be long-stemmed English roses from McQueens; jewellery has to be real, and not gold, sweaters cashmere. Even the floor cleaner has to come from Fulham Road, moisturiser from Space.NK, toothpaste from an obscure chemist on Wigmore Street. 'Why don't you get things from Boots like normal people?' he asked as he trailed round after me in Planet Organic. I am looking forward to having a boyfriend on my birthday. The two have only coincided once before.

SEPTEMBER 5, 2000
HE LEAVES ME ON MY MOST SPECIAL
DAY OF THE YEAR

The Boyfriend left me on my birthday. I know the pressure of getting me a present and being nice to me was enormous, but leaving me on the actual day was a bit extreme. I admit I wasn't very nice to him in the morning. I was about to leave for work and he was in the shower. I banged on the door.

'You could at least have got me a birthday card,' I said.

'I was planning on giving you everything tonight with dinner. I'm going to make you a vegetable korma,' he said, mid-soap.

'Well, don't bother, I'm not coming home,' I shouted stupidly.

I was annoyed because flowers had arrived that morning but they weren't from him; he made me breakfast, but only when I asked him to, and then Snoop licked my marmalade.

I got to work and spent all day waiting for the phone to ring. At

5 p.m., I rang home. There was no reply. The girls in the office reckoned he was out shopping for food and scouring London for the perfect present. I phoned him at 6 p.m. Still no reply. I drove home at top speed, and when I opened the front door I saw his keys on the mat, so assumed he was in. I said hello to the cats, who were sitting in the hallway, looking sheepish. I put my shoes in the little room leading to the garden and noticed his 15 pairs of trainers were missing. I went down to the kitchen. It was all eerily silent. There was a note propped up on the kitchen table. It had 'Liz' scrawled on the outside, and I opened it to find three sides of A4, neatly typed. (I now keep it, neatly folded, in my steel desk drawer, along with a thank-you note from my dad for his cashmere Christmas cardigan: 'I shall think of you every time I wear it – and at other times, too!') This is what it said:

'Sorry I didn't have a birthday card for you this morning, but when we spoke over the telephone yesterday I was under the impression we'd celebrate together this evening, when I'd give you your present and card, and have dinner ready. It was YOU, after all, who told me not to go out yesterday (and carry on writing my book) and I'd waited around for Robert [my sister Sue's boyfriend] to collect the bed. I would have got your things on Saturday, but was distracted by Bubbly [his teenage sister, whom he hadn't seen in ages]. Nonetheless, I apologise.

'Anyway, thanks for giving me a hard time this morning; it has relieved me of any illusion that you and I really have a future together. Your morning routine of making me feel like I'm the biggest c**t in the world (which I'm not) is boring me. If I'd the time to inure myself to being spoken to like a piece of s**t, I'd stay. But life is too short. So I'm leaving you.

'Your miserable behaviour is impossible. I don't, any longer, think I can deal with it for any period of time. Your mood this morning had NOTHING to do with a birthday card, and EVERY-THING to do with your chronic insecurity. Your losses of temper are too consistent to be due to what I did, or didn't, do this morning.

'Otherwise, you're a perfectly lovely woman: elegant, smart and witty. You'd make a perfect friend. And a perfect girlfriend for someone else, who you can relax with.

'I'm exhausted competing with your low self-esteem. I feel your anxieties daily, as though I'm treading in a minefield.

'You are 37 today. I don't believe you will relax in your ways. I don't intend to bang my head against a brick wall. As you are always telling me, you have worked too hard for what you've got to compromise – it may come as news to you, but many folk work MUCH harder than you, and don't have the designer couch to show for it. Trust me, I know a few of them. I won't ask you to change. It's best to call it a day and part…

'Slovenly and imperfect as I am, I did my best to be nice to you, without being a fawning twit. I've never said harsh words to you, and I've tried to keep your spirits high. Sadly, with little effect.

'I don't bear you any grudge. I still love you, but you are right: we are too different. I am sorry for whatever happened in your life to make you so insecure…. But it wasn't my fault. I can't be your emotional punch bag. I have peace of mind, which is a precious thing in life, and no one will damage it.

'Whatever things I've left behind, I've put in the spare room. I'll arrange to have them collected later. When, the other day, I said I was going to leave you on your birthday, I was only joking. I had no idea I would do this. I am only being honest with myself and with you. I won't carry on this way.

'I feel you have always expected this, and brought it about, to sustain your myth of how unlovable you are. Which is a shame.

'I am sorry our experiment with happiness didn't work.

'I love you.

Nirpal.'

I looked around and noticed all his books on Existentialism and the Enlightenment had gone. I'm afraid it did cross my mind how tidy everything looked. I phoned Jeremy, who was in the middle of steaming open his pores.

'No!' he said. 'You're making it up! He's mad about you. Do you want me to bike round some champagne?'

'I have been mean to him,' I said. 'He's right; I don't think I deserve to be loved. I made him hang up his towel, and told him not to scratch like a chimp. I even told him off for giving me tap water.'

I went to bed, all puffy eyed, around 11 p.m. At midnight, the phone rang.

Differences we will have to overcome

1. Age. Insurmountable: despite my having discovered a great brand called Revive at Space.NK, I am still old enough to have given birth to Prince William. I was slightly alarmed when The Boyfriend told me the Summer of Love had taken place after his bed time.

2. Race. He is Indian. I am not.

3. He is working class. I suppose I am middle class – my dad was a captain in the Army, my mum a ballet dancer – although I end most sentences with 'YouknowhatImean'.

4. I am high-maintenance. I hate going on holiday because after about a week I start to disintegrate. He is low-maintenance; merely packing a T-shirt and a toothbrush that has seen better days.

5. I wipe the shopping's bottom before putting it in the fridge. He often leaves the fridge door open, which could be dangerous.

6. I earn enough to keep me in Prada; he still has a student loan and only opened a bank account so that he could get the free CDs. He has never owned a credit card.

Chapter 14

SEPTEMBER 24, 2000
I AM REALLY NICE FROM NOW ON

Well, I picked up the phone.

'Are you all right?' he asked.

'Where are you?' I replied, a big lump hurting my throat. Squeaky shifted her huge rump, annoyed to be woken up.

'At Shivdeep's.' He told me the reason he had left was because I didn't seem to want him living with me. 'I've never felt at home,' he said. 'You were always wiping surfaces, pairing my socks... I still love you, though. Do you want to go out on a date later this week?'

The next day, I went to work with really puffy eyes, even though I had slept propped up on four pillows, like a Victorian consumptive.

'But he is so in love with you,' piped Kerry. 'You took him to Jamaica and bought him a Helmut Lang jumper.'

'I don't blame him,' I said. 'He said his sister overheard me telling him off for not giving me organic milk.'

'But we all do that,' she said sensibly. 'I told Andy's mum that he took naps on weekdays.'

I said I found it annoying that I was always leaving for work at the crack of dawn and he would sit around all day in Mad Richard's old dressing gown, drinking cups of tea and making rings on the floorboards.

'Yes, well, you did encourage him to give up his job and write his novel,' Kerry said carefully.

I met him that night on Westbourne Grove. He gave me a hug that almost cracked my ribs. I left a smudge of tinted moisturiser on his T-shirt; he said it was like dating a moth. We went for dinner at the Standard, which he paid for, and then we stood in the road and he hailed me a cab. He said he had wanted to come home on the day he moved out, but that 'I needed you to decide if you really wanted me or not'. We'd decided he would come home the next day. As I got in, he handed me a tiny parcel. He shut the cab door, and I clutched it. I watched him on the pavement, his eyes all watery, until his fluorescent trainers grew dim in the distance.

I opened the parcel when I got home. I had been hoping it might contain a ring, but instead he had chosen a pair of diamond and topaz earrings and, despite the fact that I am so difficult to buy gifts for, and that they are gold, and have a claw setting not a bevelled one, they are really, really lovely. The thought of him traipsing up and down Oxford Street with his rucksack made me want to cry.

The next day, he arrived on the doorstep with a few more jumpers. I told him I thought he might have got me a ring.

'Do you want me to marry you?' he asked, all worried.

'If I was 24, I'd marry you,' I said.

'But I'd only be 13,' he replied sensibly.

OCTOBER 8, 2000
TEN THINGS HE HATES ABOUT ME

Last night we watched *10 Things I Hate About You*, which inspired him to compile his own list:

1. Your house is a museum, not a home ('It's a 21st-century classic!' you shout when I want to have sex on the sofa).

2. Snoopy and Squeaky [he meanly called them Sniffy and Scratchy] take priority in everything.

3. You are so lubricated with beauty products at night that you slither out of my grasp, and they taste disgusting.

4. You only eat organic.

5. You make constant bizarre demands: 'Dry Snoops.' 'Hose the wheelie bin.'

6. You spend more on clothes in a month than I make in a year.

7. You made me an office with really uncomfy 1920s furniture (the desk gave my thighs splinters) and then removed my multi-coloured mouse mat.

8. You will only let me kiss you if you have brushed your teeth and flossed first.

9. You are all angles and joints – it's like dating a deck chair.

10. Your morning coffee has to be made with Illy beans, which I have to grind from scratch, and Evian. It's exhausting.

OCTOBER 15, 2000
THE BOYFRIEND STILL DOESN'T DARE
LEAVE CRUMBS

I have just got home after a gruelling week in Milan for the spring/ summer ready-to-wear collections. The thing about going to the shows is that while watching the girls sashay up and down, you yearn for a tailored pencil skirt as modelled by Gisele at Dolce, or a white jersey column dress as modelled by Carmen Kass at Versace. But then you go to the loo and stand in line in your designer outfit, clutching your obligatory Prada bowling bag, with a bevy of super-models dressed in their civvies of faded jeans, flip flops and tiny, faded T-shirts, sucking on cigarettes and reading Brazilian comic books, and you want to kill yourself, or at least take up smoking.

Fashion is an exhausting business. Not only do you have to go to shows on the hour, from 9 a.m. till past 10 p.m., you go on endless, mind-numbing 'appointments'. This involves traipsing to various palazzi across Milan, rifling though rails of clothes (green is every-where, from pea to pond) that only moments before were on the backs of Gisele and fellow Brazilian Fernanda Tavares, and waxing lyrical about everything you have just seen. It is such a closed world, where everyone knows everyone, that it gladdens my heart when someone gets it wrong. My colleague Shane recounted how, when she went on her first 'appointment', she spent ages going through a rail of coats, remarking on their wonderful cut and colour and wearability, only to be told in a whisper later that she had, in fact, been in the cloakroom.

I did miss The Boyfriend while I was away. I missed his moist eyes, his hugs, the way his hair gets flattened in the night like a crop circle.

'What did you do all week?' I asked as he lugged my case and Corso Como carrier bags upstairs.

'Fed the pussies. Watched the Mobos.'

He said he was pining so much he couldn't work on his novel, and ate doughnuts instead.

'I hope you used a plate,' was my only admonishment.

The house was very pristine, as H had just been and The Boyfriend had gone out with David until half an hour before I was due home to avoid inadvertently messing it up. 'You could have sat in the bath tub,' I said. 'Why haven't you made the bed?'

'I've never met a girl with such complicated bedding,' he said. 'I can't make head or tail of it. Most people I know just have duvets, not even duvet covers. It simplifies things.' I tell him I like linen sheets and blankets and quilty things.

'Your life is straight out of a magazine,' he continued. 'You buy tins of Italian tomatoes because you like the tin, huge lumps of Parmesan you never grate because it makes a mess and balsamic vinegar that's older than I am. And why do you only drink San Pellegrino mineral water?'

'Because I want the fridge to look nice when it's open,' I said. But I admit it. I am hard work. I want to live inside the pages of *Elle Deco*.

OCTOBER 22, 2000

WHY AM I ALWAYS GOING TO BOOTS IN MY LUNCH HOUR?

The worst thing about living with a man is that there is never a window of opportunity to grow your leg hair long enough for a really thorough waxing; the beauty therapist always tut-tuts and says, 'They are all a bit too short.' The myth about waxing is that, eventually, after many years and millions of pounds, the hair follicle waves a white flag, withers away and dies; this is not true. I have just finished reading Germaine Greer's *The Whole Woman* and she is right when she says we are worse off after thirty years of feminism. We are more exfoliated and AHA'd and botoxed than ever before, it is true, but we also have to go to work and earn all the money and go to Boots. I have never gone out with a man who earns more than I do. Because The Boyfriend is writing a novel, he never has a bean; he stays at home all day, monitoring the cats, but that doesn't mean he Brillo pads the cooker top or boils tea towels. I asked him to put up a smoke alarm, but he said he gets vertigo on stepladders. He eats copious amounts of food, things like pastries and biscuits, whereas I have never owned so much as a tea bag. Whenever I ask him what he has been doing all day, he says, 'Never you mind.' He blames the huge, warm indentation on the bed on Squeaky.

It was Little Friend Robi's 30th birthday on Saturday. I bought her lots of Kiehl's body lotion because she has dry knees and elbows. She is the one girl I know who is more high-maintenance and stroppy than I am; she won't let Deep use her bathroom because he leaves puddles.

The following night we went to a sneak preview of *Charlie's Angels*. I noticed Lucy Liu's toenails had been French manicured, something I hadn't thought of.

NOVEMBER 5, 2000
I MEET HIS PARENTS

We drive to Greenford to have dinner with his family. I am very nervous about meeting his mum, but she is lovely, keen to know when we are going to get married, even asking after the cats. His dad, two sisters and little brother were also there, and they delight in showing me pictures of The Boyfriend, aged 12 and weighing 14 stone. He still thinks of himself as that tubby little boy with a pudding-bowl haircut. It is true that plain children grow up to be much more attractive adults.

His little sister, whose real name is Sharonjeet but whom everyone calls Bubbly, is taking her A-levels, and asks me if I could give her work experience on the magazine. 'Let's arrange it between me and you, in case you dump my lazy brother,' she says, showing wisdom beyond her years.

I have a slight suspicion The Boyfriend has gone off me. On Saturday, instead of staying in bed with me until midday, he got up to watch football. He no longer emails me at work. We no longer have two-hour phone conversations late at night, although, as he points out, that's because we live in the same house. But I know something isn't right. When I was in LA last week shooting a cover, I phoned him at 8 p.m. his time, and he wasn't there; then again at 1 a.m. his time, and still no answer. When I finally got hold of him, he said he'd gone out with David. 'But the cats haven't had their dinner,' I wailed like a baby.

'I almost came home at 7 p.m. to feed them, but David has had a cat before and he said they would be okay to hang on.'

Even the step-pets are feeling neglected.

PART TWO

The honeymoon period

Chapter 15

NEW YEAR'S EVE, 2000/01
PHUKET, THAILAND

We are in a hotel on Phuket in Thailand. We are, to be precise, in the room in which Leonardo Di Caprio stayed while filming *The Beach*. I am on the balcony watching the firework displays on all the little islands in the bay. The Boyfriend is asleep in bed. Today we took a little boat to Phi Phi island, and snorkelled, which was wonderful, although I was quite afraid of drowning, or being hit by a motorboat; the fish were so curious and pecked us with their hard little mouths. I got seasick. We had a Thai massage on the beach, where small women walked over our bodies and cracked our fingers and toes.

APRIL 2001
I GET FIRED

I get home. He is standing with a tea towel in the kitchen. 'I've been fired,' I say, tears coursing down my face; all I can think of is that I must look like Beryl the Peril, that one where she makes herself up to look like a Red Indian and then is caught in the rain.

'I won't love you any less because you don't have a glamorous, powerful job,' he says kindly. He reminds me I didn't like the job anyway: always trying to persuade stars to appear on the cover, dealing with horrible powerful agents trying to get stars to appear on the cover. (Since being appointed editor I have learned that no celebrity or model is as perfect as she appears on the page: one

British supermodel has a long back and short legs, much like a Dachshund; an American cover girl has terrible acne; an A-list Hollywood star has very thin hair because she diets so obsessively – light actually bounces off her scalp; one female British pop star is as tiny as a child and as difficult to feed as a toddler; an Oscar-winning actress puts those jelly-like 'chicken fillets' in her bra. I learned this a bit too late to do me any good, but I thought you'd like to know.) And don't get me started on the fashion houses. One famous Italian designer actually videotapes the front row during his catwalk show, and if you are not actually clapping and exclaiming and giving him a standing ovation – if you are, in fact, nodding off or reading a novel while endless berets and stripy tops go by – you can expect to be thoroughly told off.

MAY 2001

HE PLAYS ROUGH

This month we spent three days at Villa San Michele in Florence (I imagine you are no longer surprised about the bank manager and the cheering). We enjoyed dinner on the terrace overlooking Florence, heady with the scent of flowers, but The Boyfriend was told off for not wearing a jacket, and he told me that, if we split up, he wouldn't be 'devastated'. I ignored him for the rest of the meal. We had sex in the vast bed with Germany playing France in the background. He splashed me in the pool and swears I was yelling, 'My eyes! My eyes!'

TWO WEEKS IN JULY 2001
HE GOES TO EGYPT

The Boyfriend says I treat him like a giant pet, which is true. His friends – Bunmi, David, Rick – think he is mollycoddled, overfed, and should get out more. I think buying him a Playstation2 was a mistake. One of them joked that I have probably had him microchipped.

He is (still) only 27, and I am sure the prospect of having sex with only one woman (i.e. me) brings him out in a cold sweat. So, I have decided to give him, if not a free rein, then quite a long leash. So, when David suggested they go to Egypt for two weeks, I bought him two giant T-shirts and a rucksack and wished him on his way. I actually dropped him off at King's Cross station.

He phoned me every night for a few days, and then there was an ominous gap. I started to get worried. Then he called again to say he had caught food poisoning from the sea (?), and had actually been delirious. 'David isn't looking after me,' he wailed. 'I want to come home.'

And so he came home a week early. I had to have an emergency leg wax, and while I was having it done my Beetle got broken into; they smashed the window and stole my CD player. I was waiting for The Boyfriend at Heathrow and there he was, really brown and about two stone lighter, and we hugged, and he smelt my hair, and we went to the car park and he got in, not commenting on the broken window, merely sitting in the back like a child because of the risk of shards, and we drove home in contented silence.

AUGUST 2001
WE DECIDE TO GET SUSIE

Now that I work from home (I have a beautiful steel 1930s desk and a tan leather Eames swivel chair downstairs, while he has his splintery desk upstairs) I have decided I want another cat. The Boyfriend, to this day, still says that getting Susie was his idea. We drove in my hot Beetle to the Celia Hammond Animal Trust in Barking. I really hate driving through ugly parts of London, but needs must. Celia has already inspected our home; I felt very nervous when she met Squeaky, who is so fat I was worried I might lose custody, but everything was okay.

There were hundreds of cats in cages, and The Boyfriend took a shine to a black-and-white kitten climbing the bars, but I told Celia we wanted a tabby. She showed us a litter of kittens, all feral, found on the Isle of Dogs; they were unable to trap the mum, who must by now be frantic. Celia thought it best we took the two tabby girls, and put them in a basket for us; they hissed wildly. 'Crumbs,' The Boyfriend said. 'The black-and-white one was really friendly.'

We got them home and installed them in his office ('Why my office?'). I named the slightly bigger, livelier one Susan, and he named the other one Sesame. (Kittens are great practice for having children, by the way: sleepless nights, endless preparation of mushy food, brightly coloured objects littering the floor, like a scratching post with a pink furry top.)

STILL AUGUST 2001
SESAME DIES

There is something not quite right with Sesame. She keeps falling off things, and won't eat. I decide, despite the heat, to drive her back to Celia's. She is, indeed, very poorly; apparently, she has a valve missing leading out of her liver. We leave her to be operated on. The Boyfriend kisses her on her tiny head, making it all wet and spiky. She dies the next day.

SEPTEMBER 2001
HE GOES TO VISIT HIS MUM AND POPS THE QUESTION

'Lizzie?'

'What time are you coming home, darling?'

'I'm coming now, but I have to get a bus to the underground station.'

'Get a mini cab.'

'I do love you, you mad old bird,' he says. 'How much do you love me?'

'As much as Snoopy, which is saying a lot.'

'Do you want to get married?'

'Yes please.'

There. That was the moment he proposed. He might not have got down on one knee, or given me an engagement ring, but he did, he did ask me, even though he keeps denying it now, saying he was 'press ganged into it', that I had 'papered him in to a corner'. But I remember that phone call from his mum's.

Chapter 16

WHY I SAID YES PLEASE

1. I love him. I trust him. He is very affectionate, always hugging me and holding my hand, and I have to say it is a huge plus point that he seems to fancy me. In my school days, I would have described his behaviour as 'randy'.

2. He loves the cats. Even when Squeaky swipes at his head through the banisters, he just says, 'OW! Squeaky darling, why did you do that?'

3. No-one else has ever come close to asking me in nearly four decades.

4. Maybe being married will make me feel more secure. Once, when I was sitting in the car outside our local Indian takeaway while he was ordering dinner, and was a REALLY LONG TIME, it crossed my mind, quite seriously, that he had just walked to the underground and gone back to his mum's.

5. I like having someone to come home to. I actually speed on the drive home and go through red lights and now have two points on my licence. He is great at explaining the plot of films (I have never, for example, much as I love it, been able to understand what people are saying to each other in *ER*).

6. He makes me feel more normal. Not a social pariah; a misfit.

7. I want to look after him.

8. I still feel quite lonely, though. There are great tracts of the day in which he doesn't speak to me, merely shuts himself in his office with the Internet.

9. I will never find another man who is so good natured he doesn't complain when I Mr Sheen the TV during the World Cup.

JANUARY 2002
HE WEANS ME OFF DAWSON'S CREEK

Nobody seems to take the fact that we are getting married seriously. Even when friends and family phone to congratulate us, they usually sound sceptical. Jeremy said, apropos nothing, 'Look at Kate Winslet.'

My Little Friend Robi said she was happy for us. 'But make sure he signs a pre-nup. He might want custody of the cats.'

My mum merely said, 'Does he still have that beard?'

We are a pretty odd couple, me playing Felix to his Oscar or Scully to his Mulder. We recently had a tracksuit bottoms and rogue socks amnesty, when he was invited to deposit offending items, without fear of retribution, in a black bin liner. I've already started to worry about what to wear on my wedding day – I never thought I would type those words, 'My Wedding Day', hurrah!! – and am thinking maybe a cream Chanel suit and Narciso Rodriguez heels (all those years sitting on a tiny gilt chair in the front row have finally come in useful). Needless to say, I have asked The Boyfriend to promise he won't wear trainers.

But, now that we are officially engaged, I have realised we are good together. He has weaned me off *Dawson's Creek* and on to reading JM Coetzee. He, in turn, has learned the benefits of tongue brushing and hospital corners. He knows that I would qualify only for the footballers' edition of *The Weakest Link*. He says he would only nominate me as a phone-a-friend on *Who Wants to Be A Millionaire?* if the topic were ponies. He is enormously kind and tolerant. He doesn't mind when I tell him that, with the amount of hair he leaves lying around and the sheer windiness of his bottom area, he reminds me of my childhood labrador, Pompey. He doesn't reach for my throat when he hears 'Mind Squeaky!!' for the thousandth time.

FEBRUARY 2, 2002
THE LOST WEEKEND

We are staying at Babington House in Somerset for three days, to check it out as a possible wedding venue. The Boyfriend didn't think he could navigate that far, so we go by train. The great plus point, aside from the wood fires, the beautiful terrace overlooking the lake, the organic food, giant, squashy beds and walk-in showers, is the on-site spa, which means I can be refurbished on our Wedding Eve.

I sit on the terrace, sipping champagne, picturing my ideal wedding day. A room filled with pale roses, a string quartet playing a Beatles song, possibly 'Something' or 'If I Fell' (I got that idea from Monica and Chandler's wedding). I'm in an outfit I saw Gisele modelling in the new American Vogue. Champagne and dinner on the terrace, with coloured Chinese lanterns bobbing in the breeze. Then we would have dancing.

But the weekend isn't as magical and romantic as I thought it would be. I had begged to be given Room 6, which has two bathrooms, an enormous bed and its own private terrace with a hot tub. I'd imagined after dinner we would sit naked in the hot tub, gazing at the stars. I hadn't reckoned on Real Madrid playing Deportivo. The Boyfriend didn't even go out on the terrace, saying it was 'too windy'. The next day, I wanted to go for a walk in the ancient woods, but he wanted to play five-a-side football with the staff. He comes back, in a really bad mood, in his stockinged feet. Apparently, he had run into a pile of rotting leaves, and his trainers smelt so bad he had to throw them away. 'I hate the countryside,' he says.

As we stand on the platform waiting for the train, he says he is going to get supplies for the journey. He returns with *GQ*, *Men's Health* and a can of normal Coke.

'Didn't they have *Glamour* and fizzy water?' I ask.

'No, they were sold out,' he lies.

But it's too late. I have already booked Babington for October 10, 2002.

FEBRUARY 9, 2002
I READ BRIDES MAGAZINE

I have bought my first bridal magazine. (I hid it inside *Elle*.) Blimey. I've never even flicked through one before, and they're a revelation. They are full of hideous ads for bone china. Apparently, with eight months to go, I should have done the following:

1. Booked the caterer, musicians and photographer.
2. Ordered the flowers.
3. Ordered my dress.
4. Drawn up the guest list.
5. Registered for presents.

I should also have posted Save the Date cards, visited a member of the clergy, and booked the venue (Aha! I have done that already!!).

Next month, I should really book a calligrapher, buy the bridesmaids' dresses, plan the menu and decide on the honeymoon destination.

'We should register for presents,' I told The Boyfriend. He looked at me as if I had said, 'We should return Susie to the cat's home.'

I persevered. 'Delia Smith says we need a food processor, a bread maker, an ice-cream maker and a palette knife.'

Brides is full of fantastic advice. It says that because I have chosen my bridesmaids (I haven't), I should let other female friends feel part of the ceremony by 'assigning them to give a reading, man the guest book or pass out favours'. Kerry cried with laughter when I read her that last bit.

The readers' letters are fabulous: 'I often get lockjaw while performing oral sex,' wrote one. 'Will this happen on our honeymoon?'

We have just had our first proper argument, by the way. The new kitten, Susie, is 'driving a wedge', according to The Boyfriend. 'Why do you have to point out every feline ephemera at every moment of the day?' he asked. '"Look at Susie! Look at Susie!" I've looked at Susie: she never does anything different!'

'Yes she does,' I said, deflated. 'Sometimes she's upside down.'

Does anyone apart from me think this is going to work out?

FEBRUARY 16, 2002
I'VE FOUND SOMEONE MY DAD
WOULD HAVE APPROVED OF

Having decided on the venue, I still haven't found anything to wear. While my boyfriend most closely resembles, now that he has grown his hair, Naveen Andrews in *The English Patient* (do you remember that wonderful scene where he washes his hair in a bucket?), I feel as old as Clint Eastwood's mum. I have tried on an awful lot of clothes in an awful lot of changing rooms with very unforgiving lighting. In Alberta Ferretti, I look too girlie. In Helmut Lang, I look like the groom.

Last week, The Boyfriend became very secretive and went to visit his parents. I didn't hear from him all day (he usually sends me text messages telling me how much he misses me) and when he returned, he'd brought with him an old hold-all. I immediately thought he intended to pack his stuff (speed garage CDs, trainers, Playstation2) and move out, but I didn't say a word. When my mum married my dad she wore a floral frock from Horrock's, and my dad was dapper in his army uniform. They were married for 58 years, had seven children, and would always hold hands in bed. When my dad retired, he would walk into Saffron Walden to do the shopping (he was too ill to drive), and my mum would stand anxiously looking out the window until he rounded the corner. He would then transfer all the carrier bags to one hand and give her a jaunty salute with the other. In the night, I sneaked a look in the hold-all. It contained half a dozen books and a tiny padded box. I think I've found someone my dear old dad would approve of.

FEBRUARY 23, 2002
HE IS NOT ALLOWED PUDDING ON HIS BIRTHDAY

So, what was in the padded box? Not, unfortunately, an engagement ring, but a pair of old cufflinks, 'in case I ever wear a shirt'.

It's his 28th birthday. He says I have aged him 'immeasurably'. We are having dinner in the Real Greek in Hoxton. He is trying to lose two stone ('I can't marry a fat person'; that was me, by the way) and is only allowed grilled fish. I am dining, as usual, off menu. I think he has an eating disorder. He once ate a box of M&S Luxury Chocolate Biscuits in one afternoon. His excuse? That it was Christmas Day.

'Do you still want to marry me, even though I'm out of proportion and can't afford an engagement ring?' he asks me.

'Yes.' I say that we can invite 60 guests. We have to work out who can come, who can share, who has kids, who isn't allowed access to a mini bar, that sort of thing. His eyes start to glaze over.

'Am I allowed pudding on my birthday?' he asks. 'And can't we just slip away to Vegas and do it? I don't want a fuss.' This from the boy who, for his birthday, wanted a facial, dinner in a trendy restaurant and a present. I decide it is better to ignore both questions.

'When you are a husband,' I say, 'I expect you to go up ladders without a murmur, mend things, know how to bleed a radiator....'

He looks absolutely terrified.

MARCH 2, 2002
I CONSIDER INVITING KEVIN TO THE WEDDING

I had dinner with my three best girlfriends tonight. Kerry has volunteered to stay with me the night before the wedding, to ensure everything goes smoothly: that there are no spiky leaves in the salad, or in the flower arrangements, and that the hairdresser, make-up artist, DJ and sitar player all turn up and don't eat too much. Robi wants to be a bridesmaid, which isn't a bad idea. I've considered enlisting for this role all my single girlfriends who are younger than me and have big breasts, so that I can make them wear upholstery fabric and frosted blue eyeshadow, but think better of it. I've decided to have only one bridesmaid: my niece from Edinburgh, Anna. She is a real beauty, with thick hair and olive skin, but is, thankfully, only 12 years old.

Michelle has offered her house near Seville for the honeymoon but I'm not sure; it would be self catering, meaning we would have to shop and wash up; far too tiring. We have been trying to book our honeymoon for ages. How can the world be full up? I asked my boyfriend if he had any preferences, making it clear we're not going anywhere near a football stadium. The other arrangements are going smoothly. I have booked a photographer, a friend who is also a war photographer; the pictures will be black and white, and a bit harrowing, but I am sure they will be fine. I am thinking of asking Kevin to be the DJ. I used to imagine him at my funeral, his shoulders heaving with remorse that he never returned my calls. But this scenario is much better.

MARCH 8, 2002
HE SCRATCHES LIKE A CRICKET

The Boyfriend asked me if I was going to convert to his religion, which is Sikh. I asked what that would entail. The no-meat, no-alcohol part is fine, but to be really orthodox I would have to be 'completely natural'. This would mean: no leg waxing, or sessions in a bright light with the tweezers, or make-up, or hair dye. If I became a Sikh, I told him, the Aveda salon would go out of business and, I promised him, with a lampshade fringe of hair around my ankles he would no longer find me attractive.

I decided to go on a dry run of all my pre-wedding honing and harvesting, and booked myself in for a vegetable colour and trim, leg and bikini wax that MUST INCLUDE MY TOES, pedicure and manicure (without regular pedicures my feet revert to hooves), anti-ageing facial, eyebrow and eyelash tint, all-over exfoliation and fake tan.

I got home and The Boyfriend wasn't there. Turned out to be having lunch with Bunmi. 'It's funny,' he said when he got back, slightly squiffy. 'She said, "I didn't know you were getting married" and I said, "Neither did I".'

That was very mean and unkind. I told Jeremy. 'There are days,'

I said, 'when I think, Oh, he's so sweet. But there are others, when he's scratching in bed like a cricket, or denying he asked me to marry him, when I want to call the whole thing off.'

LATER THAT SAME EVENING

I am feeling a little happier about things. He has finally come round to the fact that we're getting hitched, and even brings the subject up unprompted. Before getting into bed, he asked, 'Do we have a timetable for this thing?' He hasn't talked about it to his family yet, but I know they will be pleased, especially his mum. I went for a drink with India the other day and she was so excited about my getting married (all my friends had given up hope) that it rubbed off on me, and I began a flurry of wedding-related activity.

I have asked McQueens to do the flowers (I'm meeting them next week to do tear sheets, a mood board, swatches; they will cost £1500). I have also booked an appointment at Smythson in Bond Street to discuss invitations, matching map and dinner menus. The minimum order is 50, with reply cards, and will cost £860.

We decide on the wording, in simple silver lettering on white card, very plain:

Liz Jones and Nirpal Dhaliwal
request the pleasure of your company
on the occasion of their marriage
at Babington House, Babington
on Thursday 10th October 2002
at 5.30pm
and afterwards for dinner

I've made a guest list but it is a bit unequal: I have 45, The Boyfriend only has nine, and that includes people he doesn't really like. I have booked the registrar, who is very firm, saying we have to appear at Hackney Town Hall with our birth certificates (cripes!), and asking if we want to write our own vows. The Boyfriend says he will promise 'to love, honour and always use Wet Wipes'.

I have bought a bikini for the honeymoon; it is from Burberry, and cost £85. When I showed it to The Boyfriend he said, 'You'd better not stain it then.'

I haven't yet decided on the menu. The Boyfriend says that I can't inflict my eating habits on the guests – namely, no meat, fish or spiky bits, or mushrooms, or big tomatoes (only baby ones), ad nauseam – so I have conceded to some sort of wild, free-range, inexplicably suicidal fish as an option. I must remember to email the cake people about the eggs: I will only eat them from chickens who are allowed to retire. The hors d'oeuvres will have an Indian theme; the champagne will be vegan. (We were in Threshers the other day leafing through the catalogue and I chose a couple of wines marked VG; The Boyfriend thought this was some sort of Bridget Jones-style recommendation. He has so much to learn.)

The Boyfriend says he is having trouble booking the honeymoon, seeing as how he doesn't have a credit card, and that, unless he can verify 'Sade and Judie' stayed there last year, he knows I 'will have quibbles'. Hmmmm.

MARCH 23, 2002
CHOCOLATE GANACHE OR STICKY CARROT SPONGE?

I received an email the other day from my friend Tony. 'Don't take this the wrong way,' he wrote, 'but why on earth are you getting married? My girlfriend and I don't see the need: we're not religious, and we'd rather spend the money on takeaways and beer.'

It would be so much easier just to live together. I wouldn't have to visit a wedding cake website and choose between sticky carrot sponge in royal icing and layered chocolate ganache torte with fresh fruit; or between cream English garden roses and arum lilies.

Having a date in the diary when you are going to stand in front of everyone you know and swear undying love certainly concentrates the mind. Am I really sure? Even when drawing up the guest list, my single frame of mind, so long ingrained, keeps taking over. I keep thinking of single men to invite.

Chapter 17

APRIL 6, 2002
I HATE SHOPPING AND SHOP ASSISTANTS

I was in the Chanel boutique on Sloane Street today. An immaculately groomed, raven-haired young Frenchwoman hurried over on a cloud of Coco Mademoiselle. I said, 'I'm looking for a cream, well, milky really, trouser suit in silk jersey or very fine wool and silk, with hipster trousers, very low-slung: think Britney; narrow thighs and then slightly flared at the hem, like a flute, a jacket that drapes across the bust, very soft, with plain buttons, long, narrow sleeves, slightly waisted, but with a kick like a pony over the bottom. Do you have anything like that, at all?'

'Non.'

I HATE SHOPPING. I always know exactly what I want because I have seen a picture in Vogue, and I go to the store and they never have it. It is always too late in the season, or too early, or they 'didn't buy that particular look' or they have sold out. Plus, whenever we are waiting for my credit card slip to come out of the little machine, I always have a terrible fear it will be rejected, cut up before my very eyes (this actually happened in the Pineapple Dance Shop once; I couldn't stop buying Lycra), and then I will be arrested.

My alternative wedding outfit to the above is a cream, strapless, partly see-through dress by Narciso Rodriguez that I saw in *Harpers Bazaar* but, needless to say, Harvey Nichols don't have it. There are certain restrictions on what I want to wear. I don't like showing my arms, so I am also considering a long-sleeve stretch silk dress covered in paillettes (meaning it's sparkly) by Michael Kors, for $2,295; I don't know what that is in pounds. According to my fashion editor friend, sparkles are okay, as the wedding won't take place until 6 p.m. But the dress is quite short, and I am worried about people having several minutes to study the backs of my thighs. I now know why women wear long white frocks and heavy veils.

I realise I now have to worry about my make-up. I am one of those women who find a style they think suits/flatters/stays put, and stick with it. I discovered make-up pretty early on, definitely at 13 or 14, when my mum gave me a No7 gift box for Christmas, containing mascara, lipstick and foundation. Wearing foundation transformed my teenage years. I would no longer have to go into the loo at school at an angle to the mirrors, averting my eyes; oh no, with foundation I could look at myself, even in fluorescent light. I wore Mary Quant's Blushbaby in Toffee blusher, lots of eyeshadow and highlighter. I wore Moss nail varnish. I no longer wear foundation, of course, ever since Jeremy told me I always looked 'weirdly brown'; instead I favour tinted moisturiser with an SPF of at least 39 and copious amounts of Touche Eclat concealer. For the wedding I realise I need to call in the professionals, namely, a nice young lady called Sally. I call her up. We make a date.

APRIL 13, 2002
I HATE HAVING MY MAKE-UP DONE

On Saturday, Sally turned up with a case of cosmetics and a set of tiny triangular sponges. I told her I like Britney Spears' make-up: no hint of pretence at being natural, just heavy, smoky eyes, a dewy complexion and pale lips. (The Boyfriend was hopping outside the bathroom, offering helpful interjections such as, 'Shakira always looks nice.') She asked what I intend to do with my hair ('It's like a horse's, isn't it?' came the interjection from the other side of the door) and suggested I wear it pinned up, for 'a natural face lift'. I am starting to hate my make-up artist. Pointing my chin to the light, she applied a tinted moisturiser, and set to work with a liquid concealer; my face resembled a bright moon. She glued clumps of false eyelashes on my upper lids, followed by eyebrow pencil, clear eyebrow gel, and two layers of black mascara. She smeared my lips with Vaseline and dusted me with powder. I resembled Bette Davis. I asked The Boyfriend to imagine me by candlelight. The name of a Dickens character played upon his lips.

APRIL 27, 2002
DECISIONS, DECISIONS

The Boyfriend hasn't been involved in a single decision about the wedding. He hasn't even chosen a best man yet, because he doesn't want any of his friends, or his brother, to feel left out. I have asked him where he would like to go on honeymoon – Cuba, Costa Rica or India – and he said, 'You decide.' I've asked him what he would like to have as a main course: 'Pasta?' He wants to leave everything until after the World Cup, when he promises to be much more focused.

One thing he is sure about is that he doesn't want children. When I told him that I could still have children, he looked up, mouth full of Marmite soldiers, and spluttered, 'Can you? Bloody hell.' The cheek.

He said he thought I didn't like children. 'Well, no, not other people's. But mine wouldn't put sticky hands everywhere, or whine, or struggle when you put it in the car seat.'

'But you can't cope with a cat without being over protective and hysterical,' he reasoned. 'You are always sitting in front of *Pet Rescue* imagining the worst.'

This is true. Susan is now nine months old, and I still can't bring myself to let her into the garden in case she runs away and is then run over, or shot. The Boyfriend can't understand why she is allowed to scratch the Matthew Hilton sofa, or puncture the Eames soft leather pad, while he isn't allowed to sit on either in his hard old jeans.

So we change the subject. I ask him what he wants to add to the wedding present list. 'A car?' I tell him it has to come from the Conran Shop. 'What's it sell?'

'Candles. Glasses. Kitchen stuff. Sofas. Books. Bed linen.'

'Go on, then. A sofa.'

'No.'

'A book then. How about that biography of Anthony Blunt.'

'It has to be something by Nigella Lawson, or about gardening, or interiors.'

'A towel then.'

'You have to be more specific. You need to say what make, and what colour, and how fluffy, and whether it is bath or guest or hand. Otherwise, we might be given something floral.'

It amazes me how uninterested boys are in their surroundings. When I worked in an office, he now tells me he lolled around all day watching *Eurogoals* and as soon as Squeaky waddled to the front door he knew he had just enough time to plump the cushions and hide his mug. I tell Kerry we have decided against wedding gifts. 'We either sound too anal, or greedy,' I tell her. 'How about everyone gives a donation to the place we got Susie?'

'But some people don't really like cats,' she says. As if they would ever be invited.

MAY 11, 2002
HIM VERSUS DAVID BECKHAM

We are watching the preamble of the match between England and Paraguay. David Beckham limps onto the screen wearing cut-off combat shorts, a cream cardie, a woolly hat and a giant plaster on his broken foot. 'David looks good in whatever he wears,' I say, not thinking.

'Who do you fancy more, Lizzie, me or David Beckham?'

'Ummmm.'

'What do you mean, Ummm? Who would you rather marry?'

'He's married already.'

I retaliate by asking him who he fancies more, me or Jennifer Lopez. 'You, obviously,' he says loyally. I think men are realists, whereas women fantasise endlessly about their ideal partner. I used to imagine that Ben Murphy from *Alias Smith and Jones* ('they never shot anybody') would pick me up from school. But I think he was lying when he said he preferred me to J-Lo. 'You're right, I've gone off you,' he said, shushing me. In bed that night, he started to lick my chest and then started gagging. 'Eurggh, what the hell is that stuff?'

'It's moisturising, firming, and it combats the seven signs of age-ing,' I said primly.

'What, like senility, osteoporosis, loneliness?' he spat, turning his back and going straight to sleep.

Chapter 18

JUNE 2002
I GO BACK TO WORK IN AN OFFICE

Jeremy phones me. He asks me if I want to go in to work with him 'for a few days'. He works on a daily paper, seemingly for 18 hours a day, so I'm not sure. I quite like my little life, drinking coffee in the morning, reading the papers, writing. I ask The Boyfriend.

'I've quite enjoyed your year at home,' he says surprisingly (I had thought he would hate me being around, observing his naps, exercising parental control over the Sky Sports channels). 'Our little jaunts to Vicky Park, lunch at the Organic Pub, a glass of wine in the garden in the evening. We've been able to get to know each other. Plus we've been able to raise Susie together.'

I don't know why, but I say yes to Jeremy.

LATER THAT WEEK

We have just had a serious talk about where we stand, like at the end of *Temptation Island* but without the bonfire. You might think that once you decide to get married, everything ticks along nicely, but it doesn't.

'Do you want to get married?' he asked again, as if I haven't already said yes a million times. One minute he says yes to Babington House, the next he says he doesn't want a fuss. This is what he said the other day, and I am quoting word for word: 'I don't want people talking to me all day, it will be tiring.'

I have never been made a fuss of. I've never had a birthday party. (Isn't it a bit self-centred, making a fuss of your own birthday? A friend recently asked me to her birthday dinner; we had to take a present and pay £50 a head.) No one has ever whisked me off for a surprise mini-break. The Boyfriend might have paid for dinner on our first date (he keeps referring to that fateful evening as, 'The night you pounced on me in the car and HAD SEX WITH ME on our FIRST DATE'), but he has never repeated the honours.

I still haven't managed to find a DJ, but I've been thinking about our first dance. What's that one where David Byrne sings: 'I'm lazy with my girlfriend a thousand times a day'?

JUNE 22, 2002
RESPECT MY SPACE!

I walked into the kitchen the other day to find my boyfriend doing an impression of me for his best friend David. He was wiping all the surfaces with the bottom of his T-shirt, wailing in a high-pitch voice, 'Respect my space!'

I told David that, although I do indeed wipe continually (Squeaky has very sweaty paw pads), I have only said, 'Respect my space' the once. In fact, that was the first time I have seen The Boyfriend upright for weeks; he has spent so long supine on the sofa in front of the World Cup that he has developed sores. The other morning, bleary eyed after another vigil in front of the wide screen, he said that, after the final, 'there is nothing to look forward to'.

'Thank you very much,' I said. 'Only the happiest day of your life.'

I have to go to Bab House in a couple of weeks' time to go over the menu. I am going to ask India to go with me, as she knows a lot more about food than I do; the only pudding I can think of is fruit salad. The Boyfriend volunteered to accompany us so that he can 'taste things', but he has put on so much weight that I have banned him from biscuits, crisps, dairy and ice cream, nuts, Pringles and sandwiches. His downfall was that he ate a custard cream every time England lost the ball. I've told him that, even though he will be wearing an Indian Kameez at the wedding, if it is windy it might blow against his tummy. He's said the only way he will lose two stone by October is to have something amputated.

He tells me a traditional Punjabi wedding is a marathon booze-up with raucous merriment, followed by maudlin tears and, finally, drunken mayhem and a fight over the dowry. Tell me, does he seem depressed at the moment? This will prove very important come the winter of 2004/5.

JUNE 29, 2002
I WANT TO KILL MYSELF

My niece, Anna, came down from Scotland last weekend so that we could buy her a bridesmaid's dress. She brought a friend with her and, I swear, neither of them spoke to us all weekend; they merely whispered to each other. Anna is tall for her age (13). It isn't always a good idea to have a much younger, more beautiful version of yourself sloping around the kitchen, and I can only hope that, come October, she still has the braces. On Saturday morning, I went to pick up my new car, a BMW compact, bought during a rush of blood to the head and because The Boyfriend can't change gear in my 36-year-old Beetle. Waiting in reception, I see on TV that they have found the bodies of Holly and Jessica. I hand the salesman the keys to my dear old Beetle and as he takes it away I start to cry.

I ask the silent teenagers where they would like to start the search. 'Topshop?' Several boob tubes later, I manage to wrestle them back in the car and we head to Sloane Street, where we pick out a cream slip with beaded edges in Alberta Ferretti, and sparkly sandals in Gina Shoes. The shop assistant in Ferretti is really mean to Anna, telling her off for getting foundation on the dresses, and why didn't she wear a dress shield? She cries.

That night, Bruno the hairdresser comes over to give her the once over. 'Ahh,' he exclaims, 'she could be a model, yah?' He says he will simply wash her hair in organic rainwater, tip her upside down to tease out the curls, and crown her with rose petals. She sits there looking pleased. I tell her the only thing my Aunt Olive did for me was take me to Chessington Zoo and try to force-feed me ham sandwiches.

TEN THINGS I WISH I'D KNOWN WHEN I WAS 13

1. Boys aren't the be all and end all. They are people. They create lots of washing.

2. Marc Bolan wasn't in reality very tall, and would soon be dead. Marlon Brando would become very fat, and also die.

3. There is no 'cure' for split ends. The only solution is to cut them off.

4. Never moisturise your chin or your nose.

5. Don't ever go on a diet. Aged 13 I had already discovered Nimble bread and horrible diet soup that is like water.

6. You won't always be young. One day soon you will be very old.

7. Rabbits aren't meant to live in cages.

8. Mick Speller isn't worth it. He has acne. (I had snogged him at the Youth club on Brentwood high street; he asked me to go with him to see *Tommy* and I never heard from him again. Thus started what can only be described as 'a pattern'.)

9. The day will come when you will wonder why you ever wanted an afghan coat.

10. My future husband hadn't yet been born.

JULY 6, 2002
HE CONFESSES HE ONCE SNOGGED A MAN

My oldest brother, Philip, is going to give me away; he says he is going to buy a new suit for the occasion. Kerry will stay with me the night before to calm my nerves, and in the morning make sure the flowers turn up, arrange the seating plan (I am trying to seat my single girlfriends next to suitable men, or at least ones with bank accounts), supervise the flowers on the cake…. That leaves the best man. I tell The Boyfriend he should ask David, seeing as they talk on the phone for about three hours a day 'What would he have to do?' he asks doubtfully.

'Arrange the stag night, look after the rings, take charge of your going away clothes, make a speech without swearing and referring to our age difference, stop leading you astray… On second thoughts, why don't you just marry him?'

When we first started going out, The Boyfriend told me he had been away to Turin with a male friend, Patrick, a film-maker, for the weekend. ('Contrary to what you might think,' he had said, 'I did have a life before I met you; I wasn't a newborn, I had eaten basil and I had, actually, had lunch at the River Café.') He told me that Patrick was gay, and that they had snogged in a nightclub. 'But I'm not gay,' he added kindly. 'I didn't have a, you know, reaction in my nether regions.' I was relieved, but I hadn't really doubted his sexuality. He likes Spurs, porn, mess, doesn't care which pair of socks he puts on, and remains dry-eyed during *ER* (although, later, *Seabiscuit* made him quite moist).

Soon after we had started going out, I asked him how many women he had slept with. 'Four,' he said. 'Five including you.'

He asked me the same question. 'Three,' I said. 'Four including you. Two of those in one weekend.'

I have started to discover how competitive women are when it comes to getting married. I bumped into an acquaintance called Charlotte at the gym the other day; she showed me her engagement ring, which has a blue gem the size of her head, and told me that for her honeymoon she is going to trek on horseback across the desert in Jordan with Bedouins following behind carrying their huge tent, rugs and delicious food. She and her fiancé are also building a house in Thailand as a wooden love nest. I don't yet have a ring, The Boyfriend can't pay for the honeymoon, and his spectacular belches frighten the two tabbies.

The invitations arrived the other day, which was very exciting; they look really crisp and plain, although a few have already been spoiled by Squeaky, who likes to sit on any available piece of paper. I asked The Boyfriend how many he needed. 'Go on, then, bung me a couple,' was all he said.

Chapter 19

JULY 20, 2002
THE BIG DAY LOOMS

I have decided to delegate a few tasks. Robi has to organise the hen night, and Kerry, in her neat handwriting, is to address the invitations and find a sitar player and a DJ, one who is open to suggestions rather than one who plays hard house when you go up to request Prince. (The first song I ever snogged to was 'All Right Now' by Free. It was at Brentwood High's school disco, and I can't remember the boy's name, only that he had curly hair like Marc Bolan. I was wearing a tonic skirt and brown platforms from Freeman Hardy Willis. There was then a bit of a worrying gap before the next snog came along; approximately around the time The Young Disciples released 'The Road to Freedom'.)

I have a worryingly long To Do list. Over the next eight weeks, I have to buy my mum's outfit (she wants something navy, with piping), have a trial run with Bruno, interrogate a cat sitter, buy my outfit, post the invites, tell The Boyfriend how old I am....

The guests are already making demands; this isn't helping. Here is an email I have just received from Robi: 'Lizzie, can you tell them I must have synthetic pillows and duvet; and will there be any ducks or chickens walking around?' My sister Sue phoned to ask if a barrier could be erected around the lake so that her little boy, Joe, doesn't fall in. Beverley emailed to say she is still allergic to big tomatoes.

I get home from work and his face is at the window, all expectant; he has made pasta and salad. Here is an email he sent today:

'I'm sorry I didn't phone about the train... will do so today. What shall we call ourselves? Jones-Dhaliwal? Am feeding the pussies. What time will you be home? Chat soon, Plumpy. Love you...xx'

AUGUST 10, 2002
WHY AREN'T I MARRYING A BANKER NAMED STRIKER?

I still haven't found anything to wear. I just feel stupid in a dress; my head looks wrong. I have decided it's fatal to ask for advice: people keep telling me where to shop, where I can get something embroidered; the name Jemima Khan keeps cropping up. I just want a soft, fluid, milky trouser suit. I am depressed because I have been reading about a wedding in *American Vogue*. It was held on the beach in Cuba, and was between a woman with an impossible name and a banker named Striker. They had a giant cake that was for display only; a different one was cut in to pieces. The bride wore a tiara made from her grandmother's jewels. They had a bonfire.

Oh dear. We rowed last night. When I complained about watching 'Rio Ferdinand: the Early Years', he stormed off, whining, 'You just want to get rid of me.' He was asleep in bed, fully clothed, like a toddler when I went upstairs. I have to admit I have been getting cold feet. I wonder why he wants to be tied to someone who worries about whether or not he used the shower spray. He's not even 30. He should be backpacking around South America having wild liaisons with 22-year-olds in boob tubes. The highlight of my week is *Will and Grace*. He doesn't find *Fawlty Towers* funny.

I didn't bother waking him the next day, but sent an email when I got to work:

'Why haven't you told your mum and dad the date of the wedding? Why do you never ask about the arrangements and why have you stuffed your invitations in the sock drawer? Are you back on the choccy biccies? Do you want to do this or not?'

I got this reply at 4pm:
'Plumpy. When I told you to shut up last night, I was putting my foot down. You could have asked me to turn the telly over, but as I can't mind-read I thought you were happy watching *The Premiership Years*. About getting married ... you know I hate a fuss. A full-on wedding is the biggest you can get. It means weeks of stress. I'll have to make boring chit chat with your family and mine, my parents will see what a bunch of layabouts and drunks I hang out with, and all we'll have to show for it is a lot of duff photos. It is a waste of a good weekend, when we could be there having massages and stuff. On our own. I'm going to marry you (I've never had a doubt). But does it have to be like this? Our marriage will be just about us, so why can't our wedding? Don't worry, though: if you are set on the works, I'll go along with it. I want to be tied to

you Lizzie. Come on, let's just do it. Love you.... PS I am back on the biccies because I am worried about Snoops. xx'

Snoopy has lost lots of weight recently, and just sits, like a teapot, in a corner. He has been admitted for lots of tests. When I got home that evening, The Boyfriend was in the garden with tear-streaked cheeks and a gin and tonic. 'I'm not having any bloody children, either,' he said miserably.

AUGUST 20, 2002
SNOOPY HAS PANCREATITIS

Snoop has just had an operation. They have now diagnosed pancreatitis, which is treatable; it means he will have to take steroids for the rest of his life, and eat a low-fat diet. The Boyfriend has just been to visit him at the vet's because he won't be allowed home till tomorrow, and then called me at work. 'He recognised his daddy, Lizzie.'

SEPTEMBER 7, 2002
I HAVE LYMPHATIC DRAINAGE

I have decided to go on a two-week detox: no coffee, no wine, no dairy, only fruit, vegetables, wholegrain rice and flat organic rainwater. I have been undergoing acupuncture twice weekly, and been subjected to quite strenuous lymphatic drainage. The masseur said I have the most tense shoulders he had ever encountered, and that my third eye was blind to the truth about myself, that I was, as usual, doing something I didn't want to do, trying to please other people. I told him he was supposed to make me less tense, not more.

SEPTEMBER 14, 2002
THANK GOD FOR BOTTEGA VENETA

I have found my shoes! I spotted a brown strappy pair of sandals in Bottega Veneta. They look quite classy, and cost £400, but they have a high heel encrusted with rhinestones. I didn't buy them straight away (I still have a knot in the pit of my stomach that keeps telling me the wedding won't actually take place), but I have been to visit them a couple of times. And, hurrah, I also have my outfit: a cream cashmere trouser suit hand-made by the lovely ladies at Robinson Valentine on Kensington High Street. It will cost £2,500 but, as I tell Jeremy, I can always wear it to work afterwards. The Boyfriend is becoming very worried about the expense, and has suggested weaning the cats on to normal cat food. The very idea.

Last weekend, I took The Boyfriend for lunch at my mum's and he hoovered to get in her good books. The only thing spoiling my big day is that my dad won't be there; he died four years ago. I helped my mum into her outfit: a long lilac dress with a little matching jacket. 'Would Daddy have liked it?' she asked, sitting down on the bed, all sad and nervous.

Things are picking up pace: Kerry is now auditioning sitar players. The Boyfriend has now told his parents, who are very pleased, and it has been interesting listening to his conversations in Punjabi, littered with English words like 'email' and 'offside'. All his friends have sounded pleased (particularly Bunmi, who says I am 'a good woman'), all except David's girlfriend Danielle, who said we seem very different and that I am 'reserved and well dressed', and Shivdeep, his best friend from school (The Boyfriend says they used to wank together behind cushions). Shivdeep has said he won't be coming as he has his doubts. What does he mean?

Here is the menu, or Le Menu, as Basil Fawlty would say:

Indian Canapés and Champagne on the Terrace

*Asparagus Tips or Buffalo Mozzarella
with oven-dried Tomatoes*

*Roast Lamb and Braised Fennel or
Pappardelle, Cherry Tomatoes and Feta*

Raspberry Crème Brûlée

Champagne and Chocolate Cake

The Functions Manager is beginning to tire of my constant demands; she has yet to reply to the question of whether the buffalo was allowed to keep her calf.

The Events Manager has asked what to serve all the junior guests, so we have added chips and chicken, free-range, obviously. She asked if we'd need babysitters. I assumed the babies would be parked in their rooms and just left, but apparently not. The Boyfriend is in charge of room allocation, because of his GCSE in maths. Anyone under 5ft 2in gets a cot.

We have decided that Jeremy will deliver a (carefully censored by me) speech, and I've told The Boyfriend that he will need to say something too. 'What will I have to say?' he moaned.

'You have to thank everybody,' I said.

An hour later, he came back with a piece of paper on which he had scrawled, 'Cheers, Kerry.'

'No. No. You have to thank everyone – my mum, your mum, the bridesmaid – and tell everyone why you fell in love with me.'

SEPTEMBER 2, 2002
I STILL HAVEN'T TOLD HIM HOW OLD I AM

We go to Aldeburgh for the weekend to get away from it all. Our first argument is on the A12, near Leytonstone. He is driving and, although I say, 'Go straight over the roundabout and take the A12', he veers into another lane and heads towards Southend. It is like sitting in a car with Maureen from *Driving School*.

I am already tense, because we are leaving Susan overnight for the first time. I've left the cat sitter several sheets of A4 instructions, including the words 'on no account', 'a choice of', and 'in an emergency'. The Boyfriend says he has to regain his nerves, so we stop at a service station and swap seats. Instead of looking at the map, he plays with the CD changer and keeps pushing in the cigarette lighter.

We get to the hotel, and it is so full of old people it has a stair lift. We go for a walk on the beach, but I have low blood sugar. During dinner in the restaurant all I can think of is that I still haven't told him how old I am. The next day, we drive (Okay, he drives, with strangled shouts of 'Mind the hedgehogs!' coming from the passenger seat) to Southwold for lunch. I say it is too windy and the pebbles are spoiling my shoes. He says he is NEVER, EVER going anywhere with me ever again.

SEPTEMBER 9, 2002
THE BEST MAN BECOMES CROSS

The Boyfriend is on a two-week detox in order to fit into his Gieves and Hawkes tux. His diet consists mainly of pear. When his best man heard about his regime, I received an angry email:

'Now he's got the perfect excuse not to have a drink on Saturday night! As a consequence of his ever-decreasing spiral into new man, new age, new wuss alcohol-free sucker, he has suggested we go to a juice bar for his stag do. Is he for real? Anyway, now I'm determined to find him a drug-free, wheat, gluten bloody flavour-free communist lesbian disabled Romanian asylum seeker stripper. Will this gathering actually count as a stag do? I've organised wakes that have been more entertaining. Anyway, the plan is for he and I to do footie in the afternoon, followed by post-match drinks, then on to the Real Greek for a meal, when we will be joined by Bunmi. I figure we'll hit the Electricity Showrooms after that. Will you be wearing the pants at your wedding?'

Chapter 20

SEPTEMBER 26, 2002
THE DAY WE HAVE OUR JERRY SPRINGER MOMENT

It is now just two weeks before the BIG DAY. I have already been down to Hackney Town Hall with both our birth certificates and passports, but to no avail. The big lady behind the computer was quite insistent we both have to make an appearance for the banns to be put up, and for her to send the necessary paperwork to the registrar. I haven't been able to sleep; my brain veers between thinking it's not such a big deal, what is three and a half years, I don't really look that different from summer 1999, and thinking, oh God, he is going to call it all off. How could I not have told him already?

So, this morning, he drove me to Bethnal Green underground station. As we were sitting in my car before I got out, I told him I had a confession to make. 'What is it, Lizzie? You're not ill are you?'

'No, it's just that I am slightly older than you think I am.'

'How much older?' He looked panicked.

'A couple of years.'

'What year were you born?'

'Umm.' I am trying to do maths in my head, never a good plan.

'No, come on, just how old are you?'

'I am three and a half years older than I said I was.'

'Blimey. Well, that changes a few things.'

'What, why does it?'

'Well, you won't be able to have children in a few years' time, and I might want to wait.'

'But you said you didn't want children,' I squeaked quietly.

'Listen. It's all right; you go off to work. I still love you.'

I got to work and felt so relieved. Jeremy wondered what had come over me, as I am normally miserable until I have eaten my Prêt A Manger croissant and drunk two gallons of Americano coffee. The Boyfriend phoned me later that morning.

'Chubby?' (He has started calling me this as some sort of ironic joke.)

'Yes?' I asked cautiously.

'You're a silly one. But I'm afraid I was so shaken up I pranged the car on the way home. Oh, and I dug out your passport and checked it when I got back. Just in case you were really 50.'

This day will come back to haunt me later, in a VERY BIG WAY.

OCTOBER 9, 2002
IT IS OUR WEDDING EVE

We had a hellish journey down here. We got lost many times, mainly because Somerset stupidly has a place called Wells AND a place called Mells. And because I think Kerry, who was in the front seat navigating, forgot one sheet of the AA instructions. The Boyfriend was in the back seat reading a Michel Houellbecq novel. We arrived hours late. The Boyfriend said it was like 'the blind leading the mad', and disappeared to the bar for a stiff G&T. Kerry loves her room, Room 5, as it is huge, although the bath at the foot of the bed might cause a few problems when her roommate, Bunmi, a militant black lesbian, gets here the next day.

We have dinner in the log room. I realise I haven't budgeted for this. We then play pool until midnight. Kerry disappears to phone her boyfriend. We go to bed, but not until I have applied cuticle cream, plumping lip balm and Revive under-eye Emergency Repair. I am so excited it feels just like Christmas Eve when I was child, only without Morecambe and Wise.

The plan is that I will be woken at 10 a.m. with coffee and the people with the flowers; then the pedicurist and manicurist will turn up, closely followed by hair and make-up. Anna should be here by lunchtime (being a teenager, she will already have ironed her hair and applied blue eyeshadow and foundation; we will have to wrestle her to the ground and minimalise her). Then, at 5.15 p.m. Philip should arrive to take me downstairs to the big room overlooking the parkland. Kerry will hopefully have herded everyone. The rings will be nestling in the best man's hanky. I only hope I can walk in my sparkly heels.

OCTOBER 10, 2002
OUR WEDDING DAY

Well, we did it. The actual day went by in a blur, I'm afraid (the magnum of champagne we opened over breakfast didn't help), but here are some moments I remember.

Sitting in our crowded room (it was like that scene in *A Night at The Opera*, when everyone crams into the Marx brothers' cabin), having my hair straightened. My niece slipping on her dress, looking like an angel. The Boyfriend, leaning crazily over our roof terrace, G&T in one hand, fag in the other, yelling down to his family, who had just arrived in a mini bus. A text from Jenni in her Mazda sports car, saying she can't find the M4. Pulling on my outfit, and walking into the room on Philip's arm, Kerry bringing up the rear, and seeing The Boyfriend standing by the window all handsome and shy. The room smelled of roses, and there were candles everywhere and Kerry had obviously poked the sitar player into action. My future husband took my hand. I kept looking round to see my mum, slumped in the front row, and her little crumpled face.

I am now a Mrs. I have a husband. How weird is that?

We walked down to the terrace. My friend Frances, the only person I am still in touch with from high school, came up to me. I told her I still couldn't believe she only washed her Aertex top once a term. 'I can't believe you've actually got married,' she shouted, stepping over her two small children as if they were cat's cradles.

I caught sight of my husband kneeling down next to my mum (Philip and my brother Nick, the one who still dresses as though it was 1972, carried her down the stairs). 'All right, Mummy Jones?' my husband asked gently. 'How do you like your enormous new son?'

OCTOBER 11–18, 2002
OUR HONEYMOON

I am writing this in a remote cottage in the hills outside Seville; woods full of hooting owls surround us. There is no TV, no newspaper, no radio, no central heating. It is freezing, but luckily my husband once went on a field trip to the Black Mountains in Wales and learned how to make a fire. We are amusing ourselves by playing Trivial Pursuit (which you would think I would win, seeing as the subject matter is the eighties; only later do I discover that he was reading the correct answer on the back of the card as I held it up to read out the question) and chess. I am reading Donna Tartt's new book, which makes me miss the pussies. I am worried about my cheque to Babington House bouncing, and have hidden my mobile phone. The Husband spends his days thinking up ways in which we can get to watch the England game. He keeps laughing about the fact that Rick was so drunk at the wedding ('He was drunk at dinner, Lizzie,' said Robi) he started to grab people's ankles on the dance floor so he could be pulled around. He almost fell in the lake and so The Husband and David had to carry him up to his room. He was found sitting in his shower the following morning.

I can't swim in the pool because there is a giant lizard at the bottom. The Husband turns up to fish it out with a net. He has become quite manly now that we are married, and we agree he is going to have to be more proactive. At the airport, I told him I was leaving the car hire and the driving to him. 'No probs,' he said. The lady told him that, as he had passed his test less than a year ago, he would not be able to drive, at all. 'Here you are, Plumpy,' he'd said cheerfully, plopping the keys in my palm. 'Let's get this show on the road.

PART THREE

Happy Ever After...?

Chapter 21

OCTOBER 20, 2002
THINGS HE HAS NEVER DONE DESPITE BEING MARRIED

1. Paid a bill.
2. Cleaned the bathroom sink.
3. Voluntarily given up his bath towel.
4. Learned how to change the central-heating timer, or indeed how to switch the heating on or off.
5. Acknowledged Valentine's Day.
6. Picked me up from work to take me out to dinner.
7. Ironed a tea towel or cleaned the fridge.
8. Successfully applied for a Sainsbury's Reward Card.
9. Damp-dusted the light bulbs.
10. Booked anything: restaurant, mini break, flight...

Chapter 22

OCTOBER 21, 2002
I HAVE POST-TRAUMATIC BRIDE SYNDROME

We are back home. Finally. We couldn't get my car out of the airport car park because all my credit cards were maxed out. The honeymoon was a disaster. The road to the little house in the mountains was rutted and on the edge of a precipice; I don't even cope in multi-storey car parks. I was frozen most of the time. Bored. Unloved. Having consummated our marriage on our one night at home before we left for Seville, he has only been near me once, and even then it was only for warmth. He tried to remain cheerful throughout, but I knew he was just putting up a good front. Why did we do it? My mum had to loan me the money to pay the bill at Babington House. (Despite numerous mentions of the damn place, don't think for one second they gave me a discount. The only freebie they gave us was a bottle of Cow Shed bubble bath, and it wasn't even a big one.) I was depressed when I got the bill and I found that one of the guests had opened a £52 bottle of champagne from the mini bar, and not paid for it, when there was so much champagne flowing all night. That is just plain mean and greedy. I am depressed because I spent all of my wedding night chatting to my Aunt Olive. God knows where my husband had disappeared to. I went up to bed at about 1 a.m. on my own. No one said goodbye to me. I forgot to throw my bouquet; I just left it on the side where it went brown. The next morning when I woke up he was not there; I later found out he had been having breakfast with Bunmi downstairs. I was annoyed that Leggy didn't hang around for breakfast but left at the crack of dawn to 'see Bath'. I am annoyed that an aunt brought us a bouquet of flowers in cellophane. It was a wedding: flowers were everywhere. I forgot to eat any cake. The DJ asked for his money, in cash, and became quite cross. I am going to have to get a loan from those people who advertise on daytime TV. Other women when they go on honeymoon are whisked places, but I had to organise EVERYTHING: the money, the car hire, the flights, the keys, the map, the cat sitter.... I'd much rather have stayed at home. At least we would have had TV. I WANT SOMEONE TO LOOK AFTER ME FOR A CHANGE! I AM FED UP. Two years of 'Is you Is or Is you Ain't', and this is what I get? I know this is really mean, and that I have only been married a week, but

Chapter 23

DECEMBER 25, 2002

B unmi is diagnosed with terminal cancer. She is only 37.

Chapter 24

JANUARY 2003 TO JUNE 2003
I SELL THE ROLEX

We are stony broke. I can't afford lunch at work. Or petrol; I sometimes drive to work on fumes. I sell my beautiful steel Rolex for £450. I join the gym opposite the underground at High Street Kensington and try to swim but am frustrated, as I seem to stay in one spot. I hate the wedding photos (I still, to this day, haven't had a single one framed). He works on his novel. Occasionally.

Chapter 25

I AM FEELING SLIGHTLY HAPPIER ABOUT THINGS

The Husband is very worried that, now he is married, he is no longer attractive to women. We were in M&S on Saturday and he caught a glimpse of himself in the shop window. 'I'm like a moving square,' he said sadly. 'Look at me. You've fattened me up deliberately so I no longer have options.'

We were leafing through the wedding photos the other night and he kept pointing out how overweight he looks. I reassured him that women prefer men who carry a bit of extra meat, because it makes them look thinner.

I told him I am not to blame because until he moved in I never had any food in the house. Now there are all these weird ingredients, like gravy granules; my fridge is home to eggs, and butter. I don't really like having comestibles in the fridge because they make it untidy (much as I don't really like people sending me flowers; they die, and then you have to wash the vase). Every weekend he drags me up and down supermarket aisles while he sources different-coloured chillies and rice and flour.

I have tried telling him that the reason he has been putting on weight is that he works from home: he has frequent tea and biccy breaks, and lunch. He only ever wears tracky bottoms. The cats all know to steer clear of him in bed; whenever he coughs or turns in his sleep, they all cling to the duvet like extreme surfers during a very bad storm.

The best thing about him, though, is that he phones me every day at work.

'Chubby!' he said on Friday.

I could hear noise in the background. 'Are you watching *Eurogoals*?'

'No, of course not... it's on Mondays. I got up literally minutes after you left this morning.'

'Have you fed the cats?'

'Yes. I take my duties as cat monitor very seriously. Who's this?'

At this point he put the phone to each of the cats' bowls so that I could guess which one was which by the sound of their chewing.

'What do you fancy for dinner?' I asked.

'You,' he replied, reminding me why I keep him around.

JULY 20, 2003
HE CONFESSES THAT HE EATS MEAT; THE HORROR

We were having dinner at Pharmacy in Notting Hill. Horrible place. On the walls were cases of pinioned butterflies; I asked the waiter if they were real and he assured me that they were. Oh dear. I cannot be party to killing insects. The Husband suggested that perhaps they committed suicide. There was only one vegetarian option on the menu and it contained wild mushrooms, which I hate; they make me go all hot. The Husband chose lamb. 'I read a piece about the chef, and the lamb is free range, from the Welsh mountains,' he said, desperation creeping into his voice.

'I thought you were vegetarian,' I said, accusingly.

'I was, for years and years, and my mum and dad are,' he said, as if that was any defence. ' But I love lamb. And sausages.' The couple on the next table pricked up their ears; they probably thought he was confessing to an affair.

'I can't believe you eat lamb,' I said. 'Poor thing, there it was thinking it was growing up and getting fit by hiking up hills, and then it was dead. What else?'

'What do you mean, what else?'

'What else haven't you told me?'

'Well, I smoke occasionally, but not in the house. I've been trying to pick Susie up during the day.'

I sat, open-mouthed. 'How dare you frighten her and abuse her civil rights!'

'Come on, Lizzie,' he said, smirking. 'There are probably LOADS of things you haven't told me yet...'

Chapter 26

THINGS I HAVEN'T TOLD HIM

1. I fancied Kevin more. I wasn't staring at my future husband at the awards ceremony; I was hoping to spot Richard Blackwood. I hedged my bets with The Husband because he seemed keen, he returned my phone calls, he once went, unprompted, to buy strawberries in Sainsbury's, which is a really long and noisy walk, and I didn't want to hurt his feelings.

2. I have grey roots.

3. I worry that he has gone off me, even though we are newly-weds.

4. I got a loan from the daytime TV people.

5. I wish I had never sold my Beetle.

6. I once spent £10,000 on my teeth.

AUGUST 3, 2003
I DO NOT HAVE BABY HUNGER

Aren't newspaper headlines depressing? There was one in the paper the other day that read: 'Women pining for babies they leave too late.'

Apparently, any woman over the age of 35 is suffering from baby hunger; they coo longingly at toddlers in supermarkets and hold up weeny T-shirts covered in penguins in Baby Gap wailing, 'I wish I could spend all my money in here rather than Prada!'

Hmmm. People keep asking me if we are going to have a baby, or at least try for one. But I really do think I have left it too late; if not biologically, then lifestyle-y. I love my weekend lie-ins. I love silence. I love my little nephew Joe, but quite often I will tell him to shush when I am watching *Dawson's Creek*, and won't let him change channels.

Having a baby isn't something I have ever thought about. I never had dates, let alone unprotected sex. I remember the scandal when Posh Georgia at school had an abortion aged 15, and Slutty Babs actually went through with it and had a baby. At the time I had thought, Eeuuuww, how terrible, Babs has ruined her life – now who will have her; how will she go to uni? But who ruined their life by being uptight? I was actually known in my hometown as 'the girl least likely to'. The naughtiest thing I ever did was go to see *That'll be the Day* (God, David Essex was gorgeous). I wish, I wish, I wish I'd been naughtier. (Actually, I did have six months of quite vigorous unprotected sex with Mad Richard in my early thirties and never got pregnant, and the fault wasn't his as he already had a daughter with a Russian model. So I never assumed it would happen for me, same as I thought I would never get married. I had resigned myself to not being normal.)

Having a baby all seems like too much hard work. My sister used to watch every episode of *thirtysomething*; only now that Joe is five is she starting to catch up with *Friends*, series one. And I know that even though The Husband thinks he is a New Man (he flosses; he cried at *Seabiscuit*, remember), all the work would fall to me. Factor in the fact I spent most of my fertile years at work (what on earth for, I can't help asking myself) looking down my nose at women who would hare off at 6 p.m., carrier bags in hand and expressions of extreme stress on their faces, then, no, I don't think motherhood is going to cover my walls in pastels.

AUGUST 10, 2003
I THINK HARD ABOUT LICKING
JUSTIN TIMBERLAKE'S FACE

I have discovered that being a married woman doesn't stop you having insane crushes on men. I have thought long and hard about licking Justin Timberlake's face, and ironing his white tracksuit. There is, of course, David Beckham. That crooked smile, that honed tummy, the obsessive–compulsive disorder that means he is also very tidy. And then there's Damon Albarn. He looks like the kind of person who rescues spiders from bathtubs. The Husband keeps asking me impossible questions, such as, 'Who is better looking, Lizzie, me or Alessandro Nesta [the raven-haired AC Milan centre half]?'

But I am trying to grow up, I really am. I know I will never go out with any of these men and that I have a man of my own. I realise that if I had actually married Prince he would have been very annoying, smudging the pillow with his mascara and playing loud music.

AUGUST 17, 2003
HE IS NOT FULFILLING HIS DUTIES
AS A HOUSE-HUSBAND

Now, I am sure an awful lot of working women out there would dearly love to have a house-husband. They sit at their desks and daydream about returning to a gorgeous, sensitive man dressed in a pinny and clutching a Wet Wipe, poised to offer a cranial sacral massage. With a summer vegetable risotto simmering on the stove, he would be relaxed, attentive, full of questions about your day and ready with a sympathetic ear.

The reality, I have to report, is very, very different. I go off to work each morning, often before dawn, leaving the house a pristine temple to tidiness. There are new J-cloths in every sink, clean linen on the bed, The Husband's trainers have been thoroughly aired, and all the food in the fridge has had its bottom wiped. But, oh, what a different scene greets me when I return some 14 hours later. Strange mugs lurk in the bathroom. Socks roost pungently on radiators. Open newspapers are on the kitchen table. There are ghastly overhead lights on. The dishwasher has failed to be unloaded, the washing hasn't managed to crawl over to the tumble dryer. When we first started going out I would hear a mad clattering as I put my key in the door. Kerry often said that if he phoned the office and I had already left, wild panic would enter his voice. Now we are married, he makes no pretence at doing any housework at all.

He said he would look after the garden, and made a big show of devoting one Sunday to the task. After a few hours' hard labour, he collapsed on the sofa (in the same clothes he had been gardening in, I might add) and said, 'Thank God that's over for another year.'

And what is it about men and fresh air? I return home on a

stifling hot summer evening and every window is bolted shut and the back door locked. He says I enjoy cleaning but I don't. I minimise mess. I like to sleep like a cadaver so that I don't have much bed-making to do. I use the end of my T-shirt to touch the steel appliances so that I don't have to buff them with a special spray Jeremy bought for me from an obscure web site.

I have tried asking him to complete tasks, but nothing seems to work. If I send him shopping he refuses to take a list ('It's emasculating') and so he returns with half the things we need, plus lots of extra-curricular things we don't, such as those blasted gravy granules and own-brand conditioner. He says he can't do DIY because of his fear of ladders. He loses towels. How can you lose a towel? Some of his CDs are most definitely in the wrong cases. ('I know,' he said, mocking me. 'I don't know how I sleep at night.') He doesn't know how to open the bonnet of a car ('There's no need') and refuses to drive on motorways. I told him it's like being married to a giant child who never goes to school.

'What would you prefer,' asked Leggy over drinks on Monday, 'a house straight out of *Elle Deco*, or a loving, cuddly if rather messy husband?' (You have to bear in mind at this point that she is Italian.)

Chapter 27

AUGUST 24, 2003
I MIGHT HAVE TO LOSE THE NIGHT MITTS

I had thought, stupidly, that, being married, I would be able to slack off on the old beauty routine. Are all women as high maintenance as I am, or have I just been cursed with a particularly unruly body? But I find I can't do it. I simply cannot relax and let go. I have had the words 'only file in one direction' and 'exfoliate daily' and 'always use conditioner and a wide-tooth comb' and 'never, on any account, go out in broad daylight' drummed into me for so long that I have to keep using hand cream, and night serum, and neck cream.... While I am applying all of this stuff, The Husband is hopping around on one foot (all he does is brush his teeth with a NON-ELECTRIC tooth-brush and then spit in the toilet) moaning, 'Come on, will you? You don't need all that stuff. You're fine just as you are....'

Trust me: I am not fine as I am. If I had smoked and drank, stayed up all night and gone through child birth and not always taken off my make-up or lived within a two-mile radius of Space.NK, I would probably look a bit more weather beaten, but would I also be happier? Was Naomi Wolf right after all? Ye gods!! I have promised him I am going to loosen up a little, maybe lose the night mitts and the Bliss Softening Socks.

AUGUST 31, 2003
MORE MINI-BREAK HELL

On Saturday morning, we drove down to my friend Bobby's clap-board cottage near Camber Sands in Sussex. The Husband would be dispatched on Monday morning to catch a train home to take over cat-monitoring duties from the sitter, and I would stay behind all week to revel in the salty air, lie in the garden reading *Brick Lane*, and walk along the dunes. It was all going to be perfect. I would be less stressed from work – the mad drive across town to get there in time for 10 a.m. conference, when I and all the other journalists on the paper talk about what stories to run the next day: 'She's got cancer and she's only 32 and she's leaving behind two children under five; that's terrific!' – and we could have some 'quality time' together. At least, that was the plan.

On Saturday night, after a particularly strenuous session on Bobby's bed that made me worry about the mattress, we tried to book a table at seafront restaurant The Place: it is like a Conran restaurant, all blond wood, organic squash, olive-oil mash and bored teens as waiters. They were fully booked and so, reluctantly, we had to go for dinner instead in Rye. This, unfortunately, is where I started to become difficult. As soon as we were seated, I remarked that it was like being transported back to the seventies: there were things on the menu like prawn cocktail and melon with ginger, and giant wagon wheels (the real things, not the chocolate ones) hanging on the walls. The Husband had started out trying to be patient, but now he was just plain cross. I was reminded of the look on my dad's face when he had driven, pre-motorway, a gaggle of children (me, Sue, Tony, Lynnie, Nick) down to Sidmouth in Devon for a week, and all we did on arrival was moan about the cold, the gradient of the road and the smell of gas in our flat.

'But I wanted us to go for long walks and eat delicious picnics out of wicker baskets and sit on rugs on the sand, and today it was windy and people walked around holding beer cans and now you are asking me to eat baked Alaska.'

He already knows to his cost that I am a bit of a princess. Yes, I do like nice things, like Acqua di Parma bath oil. But if you have spent your life in preparation for weekends like these, you want it all to go swimmingly. And that is an awful lot of pressure.

'Life isn't perfect, Lizzie,' he said. 'Just because Kate Moss hasn't eaten here doesn't mean it isn't lovely. Why not just try to enjoy it?'

Chapter 28

To understand the huge weight of expectation that rests upon this otherwise insignificant date, I have to put it into a little bit of historical perspective. Let me itemise the presents I have given various men over the years, including, most recently, The Husband.

1. Two Technics decks.

2. A Ralph Lauren dressing gown, plaid, and cashmere sweater.

3. A season ticket to Spurs.

4. Gym membership to Holmes Place.

5. A car.

6. Petrol.

7. A rather nice £600 bicycle with all its bits and bobs.

8. An Apple G4 laptop with wireless technology and Microsoft Word.

9. A white Paul Smith shirt, and a navy Polo shirt.

10. A Rolex watch (admittedly, he didn't want it and it went back).

Now let me itemise the various gifts I have (often belatedly and begrudgingly) received.

1. A twig pencil. (The conversation went something like this: 'What is it?'

'It's a twig pencil.'

'Which is?'

'A twig that is also a pencil. You're into the environment, I thought you'd like it.')

2. A white bear bought on the company credit card at a petrol station and flung on to the back seat, narrowly missing my head.

3. Horrible flowers with gypsophilia and spiky bits and funereal dark green leaves, probably purchased from the same venue as Gift Number Two.

4. An orchid in a horrid pot, bought with my credit card.

Last year, under immense pressure, The Husband, who was still The Boyfriend and technically on probation, bought me a toy cat. I still have it in front of me on my computer (for it is very small). It is wearing a white fur stole (knowing Ridley Road market, it is probably REAL fur from a poor animal skinned alive in China), a leopard-print pillbox hat and stilettos with a leopard-print trim. Even the cats have failed to wrestle it to the floor and pull it to bits; they ignore it with a great deal of fear in their eyes. When he gave it to me, I thought it was a joke gift until the real one arrived, like a diamond-and-platinum engagement ring. But, sadly, no.

Earlier this week, I started to prime him. 'I'm not joking when I say I want a proper present.'

'Like what?' he asked.

'A really romantic dinner.'

'I could cook pasta. I can't take you out to dinner as I haven't got any money.'

'Well, you're going to have to borrow some. Try your parents.' I can see him thinking, hmm, that's a possibility; I don't know what his dad does for a living, but his mum is a cleaner at Heathrow airport.

This morning, I was getting ready for work at the crack of dawn, ironing my hair and my Helmut Lang shirt and digging out my Bottega Veneta shoes (Jeremy had promised to treat me to lunch), when he emerged all bleary-eyed in his dressing gown. 'When I get my book deal, and am a European literary sensation, I am going to buy you a house in the countryside, and a horse, and a lurcher [I love lurchers] and make sure you never have to go to work ever again.'

Chapter 29

SEPTEMBER 14, 2003
MINI-BREAK HELL CONTINUED

So, for our second mini break this summer, we went to the south of Italy for three days. I, as usual, had booked the hotel and the spa treatments, and organised the flights and transfers in Italy. 'All you have to do,' I told him, 'is get us to the airport.'

The day of our flight dawned, and he still hadn't done anything about it. 'Which airport are we flying from again?' he asked dreamily.

'Gatwick.'

'Is that near Luton?'

'How are we going to get there?' I asked, trying to keep the hysteria out of my voice (I am a Virgo; I like an itinerary).

'Bus?'

Hopeless.

Twelve hours later, having changed planes in Roma, we arrived in Bari, in the heel of Italy, only to discover the airline had lost our bags. 'I told you we should have just taken hand luggage,' he said, sitting down in the airport lounge to read *Buddhism Made Simple*.

Eventually, at midnight, we arrived at our hotel, which was gorgeous, like the High Chapparal but with expensive beauty products.

He was cheered up by the fact that he could watch Eurosport. The next day was spent happily enough sunbathing by the pool, although I noticed a certain frisson in the air.

'You shouldn't drink coffee, you know,' he said when I ordered my habitual double espresso (ever since I made him take up kick boxing in July he has been evangelical about his fitness regime; he wants to be in bed by 9 p.m. each evening so he can rise early to go running). 'That's why you're so bloated,' he continued.

I decided to let that comment slide, and entered into the spirit of the holiday by enrolling in a half-day course to learn how to cook traditional Italian dishes such as Parmigiano and home-made pasta with zucchini flowers (I thought The Husband was beginning to tire of my inability even to rustle up scrambled eggs). The teacher, an endlessly patient middle-aged woman, could hardly believe how inept (or squeamish) I am. I told her I felt really mean picking an aubergine from the kitchen garden and that, like Gandhi, I could only eat the goat's cheese if I personally knew the goat. The Husband, post-run, sauntered in halfway through the morning to lean on the kitchen counter, saying things like, 'She doesn't even own a rolling pin, you know.'

On our last night we sat beneath a loggia on the terrace eating delicious pasta that I told him might have come from the batch I made. 'I doubt it,' he said unkindly. 'You have to face it, Lizzie, your cooking is appalling. Even Squeaky won't eat it.'

I had hoped our mini break would be like a second honeymoon, or at least a first honeymoon. I suggested watching a film but he said he wanted the light off.

'I wish you wouldn't boss me,' I said at last. 'I am on my first proper holiday for a year and I wanted to let my hair down, stay up late for a change….'

He leaned over to kiss me. 'I don't think I make you happy,' he said sadly. 'You're not happy, are you?'

And with that he fell fast asleep, like a giant toddler, while I was left tossing and turning into the night, stomach lurching, going over and over what he had said in my mind: what on earth does he mean?

SEPTEMBER 21, 2003

HE THREATENS TO LEAVE SQUEAKY AND A BOX OF AVEDA PRODUCTS ON THE FRONT DOORSTEP

The day after The Husband said, 'I don't think I make you happy', we are on the plane back to London, our mini break spoilt by his bad mood and my neediness.

'What do you mean, you don't make me happy?' I say crossly, determined, as usual, never to let anything go. 'I am happy!'

'Well, you don't always look happy.'

'That is probably when I've spent an hour in a traffic jam, or you forgot to make the bed, but that is transient, it doesn't mean you make me unhappy.'

'But I don't understand what you see in me. I am a fat failure,' he says sadly. 'I know you're going to dump me. You are often cold and distant.'

'Well, okay, you are a little bit overweight, but that doesn't stop me loving you, I just don't want you to keel over and die prematurely, or squash Squeaky. And you are not a failure; you're a struggling novelist. There's a difference.' (Note here how much I encourage his writing; whenever I get him to read over my celebrity interview copy he says, 'Yeah, I suppose it's fine. It's for women really, isn't it?')

There are times, I admit, when he can be very annoying. He is always making sandwiches (so many crumbs, and knives), he can't talk to me when he is reading the papers (unable to multi-task, he says, but he can carry on a phone conversation to David while going to the loo), and he leaves tea bags in the sink. Why? Who does he think is going to transport them to the bin? I admit I can seem cold and distant, but that is because I am always tired and busy, not just from work but also from arranging for the splash-back for the cooker to arrive, or going to buy car tax at the Post Office at lunchtime, where the queues have a Russian quality about them, or taking my suits to the dry cleaner's. I get home, frazzled, and he does this game where he won't let me in the front door until I give him a password. He is all playful and sweet and I am all grumpy ('Nirpal, I don't have a password, just let me in'). Then he is hurt and crestfallen. 'When you get home from work, just for the first hour or so, you are very hard to be around. You had better watch out. One day you will get home to find Squeaky in a cat basket and a box of Aveda products on the front step and I won't let you in.'

Chapter 30

OCTOBER 5, 2003
HE MOANS ABOUT MY SPENDING

It is now, hoorah, the autumn/winter season, 2003/4. This means that on every Wednesday evening, Saturday afternoon, and quite often Sundays and Tuesdays, I know The Husband's whereabouts, and can safely take an oily bath without fear of interruption. But it also means that, no matter if we might be mid-mouthful at the

Organic Pub or only halfway through a screening of *Terminator 3*, which I was, against all odds, actually quite enjoying, we have to hightail it home in time for *The Premiership* or *La Liga* or *Serie A*.

For me, though, the new season means that gone are the barely there T-shirts and pastel hues of summer, and in their place the gorgeous new collections of designer clothes in cosy fabrics and jewel colours. I have been flicking through *Vogue*, lovingly fingering the photograph of a model wearing a moss tweed jacket – it is belted over bare skin, but I reckon it would look almost as good over a vanilla Tse vest (note: in the world of fashion, things are never merely 'green' or 'white'). The only drawback is that the jacket is £1200, but I would wear it a thousand times, so it is beginning to look very thrifty indeed. It would look perfect over my ancient Levi's, so I reason I am actually saving money by not buying a new pair of trousers. A soft bay Hermes bag would be perfect, too, although I would need to hide it until I was safely out of the house, which would have to be sold. I have been visiting a chiffon Valentino blouse in its boutique, sniffing its feathers (which I trust merely dropped off their host because it was too hot), and have been imagining wearing it on a night out with The Husband.

He cannot understand that buying clothes is something I live for, and because I purchase only a 'few, key pieces', isn't prohibitively expensive. I have never been able to tell him how much the milky cashmere suit I was married in cost, and I merely told him the caramel Bottega heels were 'not cheap', but not that they cost more than the honeymoon.

'Just because you get by in tracky bottoms and outsize T-shirts that cost less than a sandwich, doesn't mean I can do the same,' I reasoned the other day. If he starts to moan about a new purchase, I simply tell him I bought it in the eighties and that he has seen it many times before. It seems to work.

Chapter 31

OCTOBER 10, 2003
OUR FIRST ANNIVERSARY AND HE IS
IN BED BY 9.30 P.M., ALONE

It is our first anniversary. I have taken the day off work in the hope of a lazy time spent sipping champagne and orange juice, generally spending time together and reminiscing over this time last year, thanking god we are not about to fly to Seville. What with me working late every night and him, well, not, I am beginning to feel we haven't really seen much of each other lately.

I loiter in bed until about 11 a.m. in the hope he will appear with a mug of coffee or a bowl of organic raspberries, but after no sign I go down to the kitchen. He is in a tracksuit, listening to Radio 1, making himself a soya smoothie (the lid to my lovely chrome blender has since, mysteriously, gone missing). All last night's washing up is still on the table. He gives me a dry peck on the cheek that reminds me of a Thai fish. 'Happy anniversary, Chubby,' he says. Ah, so he hasn't actually forgotten. 'I'm off to kick boxing.' And with that, he skips out the front door.

I spend the day doing three loads of washing, filling the dishwasher, taking out a ton of newsprint for recycling, spring cleaning the cooker which, before he moved in, hadn't, like me, seen an awful lot of action. I then go and soak in the bath with a great new product called Slatkin Bath Therapy, containing muguet and white jasmine. He returns at approx 5.30 p.m. I tell him I have booked a table at the Organic Pub. 'Can you move it forward a bit, it's just that I'm a bit knackered.'

I get all dressed up in my Paper Denim Cloth jeans (about £200 but very comfy) and purple satin halter-neck (it cost £38 from Warehouse; I'm economising). He is wearing his pale blue Adidas top, the one I hate; the one with bobbles on the front where the cats have kneaded his chest. I drive. I pay. We are back home by a quarter to nine. He disappears, and eventually I find him on the bed, on top of the duvet, fully clothed, fast asleep. I go downstairs to snuggle on the sofa and Squeaky clambers on top of me and makes the shape of a hovercraft. I turn the TV on to a double episode of *Sex and the City*. I feel like opening my laptop and tapping out the words: 'Is it possible to live in the same house as a man and still feel completely alone?'

'It's just like old times,' I tell Squeaky, kissing her on her soft, tiny, velvety head that smells like a teddy.

Chapter 32

OCTOBER 11, 2003
DO I LOOK CONFUSINGLY YOUNG?

I am, it appears, indicative of a worrying new trend. I am independent financially (well, I would be if the daytime TV loan people would STOP RINGING ME!!!) and emotionally, and am therefore never going to be in the market for a boring old Hunter-Gatherer or even a nappy-changing New Man. I am, like Cameron

Diaz, Minnie 'I have a very wide face' Driver, Demi Moore and Sadie Frost, in a relationship with a Gardener, as those helpful twentysomething toy boys – the Justin Timberlakes and Ashton Kutchers of this world – are called. One newspaper article said last week that Gardeners are, apparently, better at communicating with older women because they '…are likely to have been raised by parents who have an equal relationship… there is no fear or mystery about the opposite sex….'

The article added that women can '…look confusingly young. You can be 10 years older than your boyfriend and still look the same age….'

I asked The Husband if he thinks I look confusingly young. 'Ummmm,' he said. 'You are good for your age, but it is obvious you are much older than I am.' He then added that he has always fancied Helen Mirren; interesting, but not particularly helpful.

I was looking at a picture of my mum the other day, holding me at my christening. She had her hair in a neat top knot and was wearing a black skirt suit, court shoes and stockings. She had probably, earlier that day, baked a Victoria sponge. She was exactly the same age as I am now, but looking down I am at this moment wearing plain Maharishi combats that are falling off my hips, a tiny black Prada T-shirt, Brazilian flip flops and a toe ring. I don't own a pair of tights, a bra, or a lipstick, but I do own the new Kings of Leon album (very nice young men). I squeeze in three visits to Holmes Place gym during the week (the only thing my mum probably did three times a week was buy lard) and drag my tired corpse from the cross trainer to the spinning class, trying to avoid eye contact in the mirrors. I go running around London Fields at the weekend to stave off osteoporosis at the risk of being brutally murdered. But maybe I am starting to look like mutton dressed as lamb. I admit I have started to hanker after the *Inspector Morse* box set. I ask The Husband if he would have asked me out if he had known how old I was from the outset.

'Probably not,' he said with remarkable candour. 'But it's too late now. I have to hang around in case you break your hip, or develop shingles. And who would bring you a ginger nut in bed?'

OCTOBER 12, 2003
I WRITE A LIST

I no longer go out. Take last Monday. A friend called to say she was having a book launch on the roof of the Berkeley Hotel. Once, the promise of free champagne would have been tempting. Now, though, I prefer to dash home straight from work, eager to see The Husband and nest on the sofa. For the past couple of evenings, though, he has been less than enthusiastic upon my arrival. The other night when I got home, he stayed in his 'office' (I use the term lightly) and didn't even emerge to greet me.

When I demanded to know what was wrong, he said, 'What do you expect? A bloody red carpet?' I hate it when he swears at me; surely this must qualify as abuse? I always thought newly-weds should behave like Robert Redford and Jane Fonda in the first reel of *Barefoot in the Park*, but apparently not. So, last Friday, as punishment, I went out for a drink with Kerry and Emine (it was like a scene from *Sex and the City*, only with lower heels).

'Will Nirps have dinner ready when you get home?' Kerry piped innocently.

'Well, he might start rattling a few pans, which are now all burnt by the way, but more often than not he is watching Channel 4 news or having a nap.'

'You are far too soft,' said Emine sagely, despite her 24 years. 'My boyfriend always makes dinner, gets up before me just so that he can run my bath, does my ironing once a week, and is very good with spiders.'

'Kevin always gives me a lift to work, changed the light bulb in the bathroom on only the second time of asking, and painted my sitting room,' said Kerry proudly. Kevin not only knows how to surf (actual waves, not the Internet) and ride a motorbike, but also has a bank account (The Husband has a Post Office savings book containing minus £8). 'What you need to do,' she continued ominously, 'is write a list.'

So, this morning, I wrote down all the things I need doing, from the new light bulb on the stairs ('But where do I find a bulb?'), to the shirts I need ironing and starching, the shower room that needs repainting and a good dose of Cillit Bang, and the car that needs cleaning. I didn't even bother mentioning things like shelves or cutlery drawers or what he could polish with Brasso because he will just think I have gone mad. He is being very mean. There was a time when he would massage my shoulders in the bath; now he just tells me off for using the hot water.

My friend Emily, who got married a few weeks before me, also has a yearning for her post-nuptial life to be all about romantic dinners and cosy Sundays in bed. She says that she and her husband, Tommy, haven't been 'gelling' recently, mainly because he has been away for three months appearing in a play in Devon, and now they don't know how to be around each other. She said that one night she sat in bed with her arms crossed, huffing. He still didn't notice anything was up, so she poked him in the ribs just as he was dropping off. 'Why haven't we been connecting? We haven't really been talking properly and I feel all alone. What is happening to us?!'

His response? 'Well, I know things haven't been great between us, but I thought it would work itself out.' And then he went to sleep.

'I think,' I said, catching The Husband mid-floss, 'that we need to spend more time together. We shouldn't have dinner in front of the Champions League, we should have it downstairs at the table, and you should light candles.'

I have been reading a new book, *Against Love*, which seems to support my worries. 'Monogamy turns nice people into petty dictators and household tyrants,' the (female) author writes. 'What is it about modern coupledom that makes policing another person's behaviour a synonym for intimacy?'

What is it indeed.

OCTOBER 26, 2003
JEALOUSY; HMMM

My policy regarding jealousy has always – until now, of course – been to date a man nobody else wants. Take my second boyfriend; let us call him T, when in fact we all know his name is Trevor. He wasn't what you would call handsome, although he had a kind face. He had an oddly stooped gait, wore his trousers impossibly high, so the waist skirted his nipples, ironed his pants and used TCP as an aftershave. He was always sloping off to poetry readings. But, even boring, antiseptic-scented Trevor managed to go off first with a very pretty 24-year-old stylist, and then move in with a small ('She looks like one of your friend's children,' I told him meanly) African woman permanently in a head wrap, who already had a child. Which only goes to prove that no matter how unsavoury the man, there is always a woman (younger, dimmer, slimmer) waiting eagerly in the wings.

Now, I have never been troubled by twinges of jealousy where The Husband is concerned. Not because he isn't handsome – he is; with huge brown eyes and long, thick eyelashes – but because he has always seemed so devoted, paying me compliments, making scrambled eggs on toast....

But, recently, two things have happened. Three months ago, when he tipped the scales at 17 stone, I decided drastic measures were in order and so I marched him along to a gym called Karmaa in Camden. There, he has undergone such a rigorous workout regime that he has lost a remarkable two and a half stone. His tummy, which had become like a member of our family, has all but disappeared, making him a lot more mobile. And he has started to comment on other women. We were at Victoria Beckham's album launch party on Saturday night, and Jade Jagger brushed past him. 'Oh God,' he gasped open mouthed. 'She looks like an Indian princess.' A couple of nights later, we went to Sadie Frost's catwalk show in what seemed to be a former car showroom near Victoria station. I never worry about him fancying models (he finds them too bony to be sexy) but I became aware that he was staring at Kate Moss, sitting opposite us.

'She has the most exquisite features I have ever seen,' he whispered softly.

'But you hate women who smoke,' I argued.

'I wouldn't care,' he said.

Kerry says I shouldn't worry. 'It's like you saying you want to lick David Beckham's armpit at the end of a match. You might fantasise about it, but it will never happen.'

But now that The Husband is out and about without the tummy, I have been wondering. Then, last night, after an evening kick-boxing class, he went for a drink with his new super-fit friends and didn't get home until one in the morning (Squeaky and I pretended to be asleep). But I so don't want to turn into one of these women who always need to know where their man is. I bet Kate Moss never says to Jefferson Hack, 'So, what time do you call *this*?'

Kerry has a great idea. 'I know,' she squealed. 'Why don't you make *him* jealous.' Hurrah! Now we have a cunning plan.

'He'll hate that,' agreed Emily. 'My husband can't stand me going to parties and leaving him at home with Bruiser and Princess [her cats]. He thinks men will be swarming all over me.'

Men have never swarmed all over me, so I very much doubt they are about to start now.

'Do you worry about other men chatting me up when I'm out and about?' I asked him in bed, when I was reading *The Bride Stripped Bare* (great – lots of sex), wearing a faded Snoopy T-shirt and Talika eye and lip mask, which you have to stick on, like a plaster.

'No, not really,' he said, using me to prop up his hardback copy of *Stalingrad*. 'They wouldn't dare.'

'Why not? You did.'

'Yes, but via email, remember?'

'Weren't you worried when I went out with Kerry and Emine and I was wearing my Alberta Ferretti gypsy top?'

'Not really. You're not really a gypsy-top kind of girl. You should stick to shirts and suits.'

Chapter 33

NOVEMBER 16, 2003

IT DAWNS ON ME: HOW ON EARTH DID I DO IT?

I have just been soaking in an oily bath reading *Find A Husband After 35* by an American author called Rachel Greenwald. Perhaps things are different in America, but I found some of the advice hysterical: take up Spanish classes; get your girlfriends to recycle their old dates; surf the Internet (very important when you are in your mid-thirties, apparently).

You might ask how I manage to have the time to read such a weighty tome, what with three high-maintenance cats, a husband who moults and makes smells like a labrador, a VERY DEMAND-ING job on a daily paper, and a fitness regime that would make Paula Radcliffe need to lie down. But last weekend I was left on my own, as The Husband went on a stag night in the Scottish Highlands with a travel company called Nae Limits. Having done all the odd jobs around the house (cleaned the Smeg using an asep-tic technique, bought a new loo seat AND fitted it myself, put all the pillows in the wash because Squeaky dribbles on them, given the cats reflexology on their paws) I sat down, all moisturised and immaculate, Diptyques burning on every surface, and it reminded me exactly what it felt like to be single. I was able to watch two Cary Grant films back to back (*The Philadelphia Story* and *Bringing up Baby*) without comment and while wearing a pore strip, and didn't wear any make-up all weekend as I was conditioning my eyelashes and giving my skin a Sisley serum boost (for use after childbirth, divorce or extreme stress); I was also able to wear Revive's Perioral Renewal Cream without fear it would be licked off.

I admit I do still wear make-up in front of The Husband at all times. And I still brush my teeth and apply emergency Touche Eclat before I drive home from work. Is this sad and anti-feminist? He thinks it means I am still keen. But, let's be honest. How on earth *did* I find a man when I am so obviously over 35, so obviously pernickety ('Hmmm, Brad Pitt, don't like his nostrils') – and such a nice, sweet, compliant man at that? Well, to be honest, I haven't a bloody clue. I had never, once, been able to rustle up a date for those important occasions – weddings, my dad's funeral, Millennium Eve – and hadn't resigned myself to singledom so much as was turning it into an art form. I did everything the glossies told me to: I enjoyed a spa day at home, pampered myself with a chocolate cashmere Nicole Farhi throw, ate mangoes. I suppose it worked because I was never lonely; I was always far too busy peeling difficult fruit.

Anyway, he phoned at 10 a.m. on Saturday morning to say the candlewick bedspread was scratchy and he was tempted to take the next train home. 'No, don't,' I wailed. 'I need my space!'

'You are such a liar,' he laughed. 'I know you are applying some dreadful unguent. But can you please not wear my T-shirt while you're doing it?'

Chapter 34

NOVEMBER 30, 2003

I HANKER AFTER GARY IN THIRTYSOMETHING

I have just got back from four days in Los Angeles, where I interviewed a supermodel and an actor for my paper. (My job is not as glamorous as it sounds. I flew ten hours in Economy, so now probably have deep vein thrombosis, then the hotel was so crumby I couldn't even get a glass of water; I spent most of the time in my room watching *Finding Nemo* in floods of tears.) I return to find The Husband has not only cut his hair, which had reached halfway down his back, but has wet-shaved his head.

'What do you think?' he asks as I drag my case through the front door.

'It's awful. People will think you are trying to cover up the fact that you have premature male pattern baldness. Like Fabien Barthez.'

'Well, I had hair like this when we met, and that didn't stop you sleeping with me on our first date.'

'I don't like it now. It looks aggressive, and you can see your spotty head, and it will be cold in winter.'

He has this thing that I am trying to turn him into the boyfriend I never had in the late seventies. 'Why else would you tell me to get a feather cut and buy me things in cheesecloth?'

I can't deny I am partial to men with long hair and weedy thighs. Seventies man – be he David Cassidy or the lead singer of Mott the Hoople – was slightly feminine; he wore love beads and smelt of joss sticks.

Although I do love The Husband, there is nothing to make me feverish quite like a dose of unrequited love. I used to dash home to ensconce myself in front of *Miami Vice*, so deep was my affection for Sonny Crocket. I also loved Gary in *thirtysomething* and was very sad when he was killed on his bicycle.

Chapter 35

SQUEAKY, AND MY OTHER FUR BABIES

I could write a book about my little black puss Squeaks, and probably will one day. I am always being teased at work about my pets; they keep saying ridiculous things such as, 'Your cats must be a substitute for a baby....'

My cats are not merely warm beings on whom I lavish my affection until a real baby comes along, oh dear me no. They are people in their own right, with likes and dislikes, favourite spots, humour, moods. When The Husband first moved in, he was given a very hard time by Squeaky, who became jealous and made a point of sleeping on his pillow ('Don't, Squeaky,' I would whisper to her, 'he's a spot head'). She has now grudgingly accepted his presence, and understands she still comes uppermost in my affections (The Husband is now fourth, obviously).

Squeaky and I have an extraordinary bond. The Husband says that about half an hour before I get home, she waddles off to sit on the front door mat. When he is mean to me (my mum doesn't believe this, but there are days when he is grumpy and uncooperative), Squeaky swipes him. She always sleeps between us, like a giant black draught excluder, and in the morning is like an alarm cat, licking me strenuously until I get up to organise her breakfast.

The Husband puts her on the phone several times a day while I'm at the office, and she chats away, getting all excited and dribbling. One of the main reasons I married The Husband was that his future step-pets took to him. I would lie in bed on a Saturday morning (his turn to feed them), and hear him chatting away to them ('Hello, little one!') and cooing softly.

Snoopy has always been a joy: good natured, shy, loving; always uses the litter tray, even when he has just been under general anaesthetic and can only crawl; overall, much, much better value than a boyfriend.

And then, of course, there is Susie. She is still kitten sized and incredibly fussy about her food: she has to be in the right mood, it has to only have gravy (she hates jelly), be in the right location.... She is a bit like her mummy, really. We joke about how much time we spend talking about the cats. 'I'm a man,' he says. 'I shouldn't be saying, "Come on, time for a tum-tum tickle."'

Chapter 36

DECEMBER 14, 2003
THE DAY HE TELLS ME TO SHUT UP

Now, if I were Mrs David Beckham, which I am not, I wouldn't let my beloved languish in a Madrid hotel room, ordering bottles of wine to drink on his own while I am having dinner at the Ivy or sitting at home ironing Brooklyn's T-shirts. I believe that if you can be bothered to get married (and believe me, it is a bother, even without thrones), then you should be inseparable. Like Paul and

Linda McCartney, or Paul Newman and Joanne Woodward.

I am always encouraging The Husband to get out more, to see the world before he hits thirty, but he says he would much rather stay home with me and the pussies. Take the stag do with Nae Limits. He has just confessed that his hotel bill included no less than £140 spent on phone calls to me, and he was only away for three days. There are moments like these that make me think, yes, he does really love me.

But then I have second thoughts. I have just had a week off work and, when I wasn't trying to sell, due to extreme poverty, my BMW (I eventually did, for £10,000 less than I paid for it, and it had only done 4,000 miles, most of them slowly), I spent most of it in the garden wrestling with prehistoric-size vines and roots. He didn't offer to help once. When I asked him, gasping, for a drink of water, he passed it through the cat flap instead of opening the door because 'it's too cold'. Then, this morning, without much provocation, he told me to shut up.

Now, everyone who knows me will tell you that I am the most thin-skinned person on the planet. In fact, I don't have a skin. I am just a mound of quivering flesh waiting to take offence. As The Husband says, I am very easily moved to hot tears. I have just read in *Heat* magazine that Brad Pitt calls Jennifer Aniston 'Leaky', so permanently moist are her eyes. I warmed to her immensely.

A LIST OF THINGS I DON'T LIKE

1. Him not looking up when I walk in to a room, then, when I pointedly say something or cough, he drags his eyes away from the TV in slow-mo; he reminds me of Kevin the Teenager.

2. Him being in his 'office' with the door shut (this is not only rude, it also prevents Susie gaining access to her special cushion).

3. Him falling asleep at 9.30 p.m.

4. Him making me watch *Matrix Re-whatever* when I wanted to see the one with George Clooney.

A LIST OF THINGS I DO LIKE

1. Diptyque candles.

2. A bottle of Acqua di Parma bath oil.

3. A pair of Damaris knickers.

4. *Frasier*, First, Second and Third Series, the complete episodes.

5. Chocolate Brazil nuts.

6. Snoopy, Squeaky and Susie (and, at some point in the future, Sweetie).

Chapter 37

DECEMBER 21, 2003
MEMORIES OF 'PAR BOILING' MISTAKES

Oh dear. Christmas lunch. Let me tell you about the debacle last year. It was our first Christmas as a married couple, and so our relatives and friends had decided to leave us alone to snuggle in our new cashmere socks. We agreed that, for the first time ever, I would be in charge of the cooking. No poor, unsuspecting feathered creature would be wrestled away from its loved ones. No. Our lunch would be completely vegan, and I would plan the menu, do all the shopping, and prepare and cook the meal. The deal was that

I would get to watch *Top of the Pops* and he would load and empty the dishwasher.

How hard could it be? I had my trusty Cranks recipe book, bought in hardback at the end of the seventies and still pristine. We'd have green salad to start, followed by nut roast with spicy peanut sauce, roasted parsnips, carrots, potatoes and steamed sprouts. Pudding would be chunky fruit salad.

I went shopping late on Christmas Eve as I was at work all day. I went to Fresh and Wild in Notting Hill, the store where you can spend a week's wages on a carefully nurtured pumpkin. I bought ethical nuts in their shells, the spices and coconut, unbleached flour to make breadcrumbs, and the carrots, parsnips and potatoes, all happy in their muddy coats. I have never trimmed and washed a lettuce (mine always comes in a pillow), so I bought two heads that I hoped were not harbouring caterpillars, which would have to be re-homed. They didn't have any sprouts – damn and blast! – so I had to crawl to M&S, and I'm afraid I cheated a bit here, and bought ready-trimmed ones, like marbles. I forgot the fruit, and got a taxi home.

I decided to make the nut roast later that night rather than on Christmas Day itself. An hour later and I was beginning to rue the day I bought nuts in their shells. Then the recipe asked me to line a loaf tin with greaseproof paper. I possess neither. I do have a metal pizza dish, so I spread the mixture on that. On Christmas Day, I got up really early and put the vegetables in the oven, but by 7 p.m. they were still raw. I hadn't, my sister told me many moons later, par-boiled them or drizzled oil on them. The nut roast, although round and thin, was nice but dry, as I was too tired to make the spicy sauce. The Husband began to look quite menacingly at the cats as they tucked into their human dish of organic turkey.

We are, obviously, going to my sister Sue's this year.

Chapter 38

JANUARY 4, 2004

A MOTHER TACKLES ME SCREAMING, 'YOU CAN'T GO UP
THERE! A BABY IS SLEEPING!'

So, the New Year's Eve party in the Cotswolds. We set off, me driving, him sleeping, along the Marylebone Road towards The Countryside. We arrived at the pub where we would be staying the night, and where we could get changed. He examined his T-shirt, and after a quick rub decided he didn't need to change into a fresh one. After several dead ends, and a heated argument about the fact that he wouldn't be able to carry me from the car in the event of mud/grass/puddles, we finally made it to the party, held in the ginormous and very well equipped farmhouse kitchen of my friends India and Andy.

Now, I don't know about you, but I am at the stage in my life when, at every party I go to, there are hordes of children milling around carrying teddies, and anxious mothers who have stashed sleeping babies in various bedrooms, and who every five minutes hand longsuffering partners their white wine and scamper up the stairs to check if their progeny is still breathing. I attempted to go to the attic floor to check out India's new wet room, when one mother tackled me, much in the manner of Martin Johnson, shrieking, 'You can't go up there! A baby is sleeping!'

'Promise me,' The Husband said when I returned, visibly shaken, 'you will never develop baby hunger. I don't think my nerves could stand it.'

After champagne, and several hours of karaoke, in which The Husband made a complete fool of himself, we drove in the pitch black back to the pub, which itself had a party that went on until six in the morning. The room was freezing. The next day, we were supposed to go back to the house for breakfast, but couldn't find it (all the lanes looked the same), so drove back to London grumpy and tired.

Having had a few days off work over the festive period (I am back at my desk tomorrow and will find it hard to concentrate, what with all the men in lurid sweaters and the women detoxing all over the place), I have been able to observe at close quarters exactly what The Husband gets up to all day.

1. He gets up, but doesn't make the bed.

2. He makes instant coffee with milk and two sugars.

3. He watches *This Morning* and maybe *Football News*.

4. He takes a very long shower and leaves his towel, full of old water, in a crumpled heap.

5. He uses Lynx body spray, despite the fact I bought him Allure pour Homme for Christmas.

6. He tries to put on the T-shirt and tracky bottoms he was wearing the day before, but as I am temporarily at home anything left on the floor for more than two minutes is considered fair game and has been banished to a hot wash.

7. He stumbles around, opening the airing cupboard and opening drawers BUT NEVER CLOSING THEM until he finds an identical outfit. He then sits down in front of the TV again; occasionally, he will sit in front of his computer to 'check my emails'.

I think he will be quite glad when I am back at work.

Chapter 39

HE BUYS THE WRONG SEA SALT

Next month, The Husband will pass the milestone that is thirty (he's a Capricorn). For the past few weeks, he has been moping about the house in a fit of depression over his lost youth, examining his hairline in my magnifying mirror. He said he feels old beyond his years.

'How?' I ask him grumpily. 'You are not at all domesticated. Despite living here for three years, you still don't know how the central heating works.'(The other day, I asked if it was timed to come on and he replied, 'How should I know?')

'I go to Tesco,' he says.

That's true. Last weekend, while I was having a marathon sleep-in with the two tabbies, he took himself off to do a weekly shop. Even though he forgot quite a few items, such as dishwasher tablets, and got a few things horribly wrong – he bought ordinary sea salt, not the one that is hand-skimmed from 2,000-year-old ponds (Rain Tree Fleur de Sel, £2.19 from Waitrose), non-organic milk, and giant bottles of fizzy water (only Pellegrino has the correct forcefulness of fizz) – I kept quiet. He had remembered the Charmin Ultra, the Illy beans and the vegan wine. He says he feels like one of the victims on *Queer Eye for the Straight Guy*, the reality TV show in which an unreconstructed man with a hairy back and terrible shoes is made over by five gay men, and initiated into the world of candles, napkins, flowers, facials and ironing.

I remind him that, despite being on the cusp of thirty, he is still very juvenile. He doesn't have a credit card. He gets up really early on Saturday morning to watch TV. When he breaks things – mugs, cat bowls, THE BUTTER DISH – he hides them in drawers. He is always whispering on his mobile. Sometimes he goes to bed without brushing his teeth.

I have to concede, though, that he doesn't have a temper. This can at times be annoying ('But they nicked our space in the car park!') and it was only recently I found out why trivial things, like a lift not working, or the lights turning red, or M&S deciding to relocate the Italian section, don't bother him in the slightest. He says his mum slept every single night in the same bed as her mum until she left India, for an arranged marriage in west London, so it doesn't really get to him whether our duvet has 400 threads or not. And because his aunties still find it hard to find water of any description, he finds my fizzy rating mildly bonkers.

JANUARY 18, 2004
HE LOSES HIS TEMPER

Having written last week that he never loses his temper, I'm afraid I am going to have to report otherwise. Last Thursday morning he proved me very wrong indeed. He was driving me to the station at 7.30 in the morning, when he suddenly said, 'Why do you have to let the alarm beep over and over again? Why can't you just set it for the time that you actually want to get up?'

I thought this was charming. I responded by gulping, 'Well, perhaps I'm tired from working a 65-hour week and getting home and finding that you have done absolutely nothing, as usual.' Then, I'm afraid I let the feminist side down somewhat by having huge, fat, globular tears roll down my face and splash on my nice clean shirt.

'That's it, Lizzie, start crying, why don't you,' he said in a really mean voice. When I got out of the car I slammed the door with force and stormed off. He didn't phone me at work all day.

The night before this particular escapade, he had said to me that maybe I could get up a bit earlier than 6.30 a.m. because he had things to do before meeting a friend for lunch and then going to see a film. Now, I don't know about you, but I thought this was a little bit rich. 'What things?' I asked, incredulous. I had just got home to find his bits of paper and old envelopes scattered on my lovely steel desk, when he has his own perfectly good office, washing-up in the sink, laundry still in the tumble dryer from about three days ago, and the house in virtual darkness (why do my light bulbs go all the time? I must live on some weird ley line).

'Never you mind,' he said. He also hadn't fed Susan. Now, I know she is difficult and squirmy and time-consuming, but she is very small and needs three meals a day and lots of snacks in between.

Maybe I was just over-tired. But when you get home from work, the last thing you want to do is take out the rubbish and start poaching cod. I rang my best friend, Jeremy. 'You are a bit prickly in the morning,' he said, not very loyally. 'I always find it best to leave you well alone until after about 11 a.m.'

I consulted my friend Kerry. She said that I shouldn't have to do anything when I get home after a long day. I told her that sometimes I delay going home because I'm worried about the mess; mad and weird, I know, but I can't help it.

'It's really not good for him not doing anything,' she said. 'He probably doesn't talk to anyone all day and when you get home he's a bit out of kilter. The less you do, the less you can do.' She is living very happily with her useful boyfriend, Kevin, although she too admits the romance has gone out of their relationship somewhat.

For their first Christmas together he bought her Agent Provocateur underwear costing over £200; this year, she got a set of saucepans.

I am about to log off, leave my desk and begin the long trek home. Will he have fed Sue and put on a white wash? Or will I get home to find a box of Aveda products and Squeaky on the front step?

Chapter 40

JANUARY 25, 2004
I HANG OUT WITH BLUR AND HE ACTS PECULIAR

I got home from work on the day of our argument about the noisiness of my alarm clock. He was watching TV, his plate in the middle of the floor. 'You've eaten, then,' I said.

'Yup. Yours is on the stove.'

I went and had an oily bath and heard him pad up the stairs and go in to his office and shut the door. I had my lonely dinner in front of *Newsnight*.

The next day, he didn't phone me until about 4 p.m., when he called to say he had left biscuits under the bed for Susie, but that I had better not be home too late.

'Why?'

'I'm at my mum's,' he said cagily. 'And then I am going to David's to drink vodka. I'll probably stay the night.'

Well, he hasn't seen his mum since the wedding, so I suppose she is due a visit, and I don't mind him seeing David, except that often he returns home a different boy, swearing and putting his feet on the sofa. But I simply replied, 'Fine, I am going to see Blur and then I'm going to the exclusive after party.'

'Good,' he said, not remotely interested. 'You take care.'

It was true that I was going to Blur's party, although I am not above making something like that up.

I had been invited to the party by my friend Meena and her two friends, Olivia and Lisa. I met them outside the venue on Elephant and Castle roundabout, and you really know you are getting old when you say to someone, as I did to Olivia, 'Aren't you cold?' Lisa was a 'newly', according to the other two, meaning she had got married only a few months before and was still at the stage where you giggle down the phone all the time and presumably don't say, 'You take care.'

Lisa was wearing a white rabbit-fur stole. I told her I had a white pet rabbit as a child, called Penny. Although I used to make her show-jump piles of paperbacks on the lawn, I loved her very much. I think I spoiled Lisa's evening. I didn't stay at the party long, despite being in the vicinity of Damon Albarn, because I was feeling tired and sad and desperate to get home and see the cats. I really thought being married would be different to just going out with someone; that the stomach-churning feeling of 'will he or won't he bloody well phone' would be replaced by something warm and secure and mutually supportive.

I recently consulted a life coach, it being January, and she looked aghast when I said he never has the house looking all nice and dinner on when I get home, and that my Christmas present had been a hand towel from John Lewis that doesn't match because it's floral. I broke down in tears, actually, at the enormity of my life, all the constant tasks. 'You aren't his mum or his flatmate,' she said kindly. 'You have to give him an ultimatum.'

But what would the ultimatum be? That he is only allowed on his

Playstation2 for an hour a day? That he will lose custody of his two step-pets and one whole pet? I don't want to boss someone around; I want them to leap unprompted.

I got home from Blur to find everything tidy, and a note saying he was taking me to dinner the following evening, and that if he stayed at David's at least I would get a good night's sleep. I don't know.

FEBRUARY 8, 2004
HE WEARS JUMBO CORD

We went to a really swanky wedding last night. One of The Husband's best friends, Imran, was the groom. I decided to make a real effort, as lots of The Husband's former colleagues from the BBC would be there.

I spent most of Saturday attending to my toilette. First, I put on a hair pack, ladled on a Kiehl's moisturising mask and sat in an oily bath reading *Olivia Joules and the Overactive Imagination*. I spent an hour applying my no-make-up make-up look, and put on my Myla underwear, black Prada suit and sparkly Helmut Lang heels. Earlier in the day, I had suggested that The Husband wore his black wedding tux, white shirt and black loafers and new black socks. I kept asking him to iron his shirt, but he wouldn't be budged from *The Simpsons*. As our taxi beeped outside, he came downstairs in jumbo (jumbo!) cord jeans, a blue ribbed sweater over a shirt, brown hiking boots and white socks.

'Why?' was all I could utter.

'I won't feel comfortable in a suit.'

'But going to a wedding isn't about you being comfortable, it's about them. It's disrespectful.'

As we left that evening, no couple has ever looked more mismatched. I told him that people at the wedding would think I was his social worker. I also told him that, just as Gwyneth Paltrow would want Chris Martin to put on clean underpants and wear something that doesn't have a hood for the Oscars, I expected The Husband to show me a little respect as well by at least attempting to look smart.

We got to our table, full of beautiful young women in one-shouldered tops and men in dark suits, and he did immediately feel out of place.

Chapter 41

FEBRUARY 14, 2004
VALENTINE'S DAY: AAARRGHHH

Having been single for most of my life, suffice to say I have never enjoyed this particular day on the calendar. I would travel home from work on the bus with other people's roses threatening to take my eye out, with nothing to look forward to but an episode of *thirtysomething* or *ER*, depending on the decade. Even during the brief periods when the two (boyfriend and Valentine's Day) coincided, the boyfriend pretended not to believe in Valentine's Day (a likely story; I am convinced that the women they went out with after me were showered with rose petals and whisked to Venice).

All (and I use that word loosely; can it possibly apply to four men?) the men I have known have been perfectly useless on this most special day. On his giant appliquéd card, Trevor inscribed the Prince song lyrics, 'If I was your girlfriend would you talk to me as only a best friend can?' I then suspected him of being secretly gay. (Actually, when I joined the glossy, I consulted a psychic and she said, and I am not lying here, that, 'You went out with someone who turns out to be gay, you will get married really quickly and to someone who is the best thing that could ever happen to you, you will write a book about yourself that everyone will want to read, and you will have four...cats.' I swear this is exactly what she said. Most of those things have turned out to be true.) Kevin wasn't around long enough to make it for a Valentine's Day, although I think I was stalking him around that time and seem to remember I sent him a card with lots of clues.

This year, I have to report that The Husband and I (!) are not as lovey-dovey as we once were. I haven't had a poem for months. He makes no pretence at preserving an air of mystery in front of me (whereas I still lock the bathroom, and screech, 'Don't come in!' if he even dares to make a shadow on the door). The other day when he kissed me he burped in my mouth. Euuwww.

Chapter 42

FEBRUARY 22, 2004
I KNOW A LOT ABOUT PETS, BUT NOT VERY MUCH
ABOUT POLITICS

I was sipping my organic flat rainwater in the Organic Pub when The Husband said something very ungenerous: 'Women are better informed than most men, but never as informed as the most well-informed men. They are not interested in politics; they find it too boring to retain what's important.'

'That's not true,' I piped. 'I read all the papers every day. I voted in the last two general elections.'

'Only because you thought Tony Blair was handsome. Okay, let's put your knowledge of current affairs to the test. Who is the president of Pakistan?'

'Ummm. Well, he has a nice house and two labradors.'

'No, that was the head of the nuclear weapons programme.'

'You are only asking me questions you know the answer to,' I said in a really whiney voice. 'Here's one for you, clever clogs. What was the name of Bill Clinton's cat?'

'I don't know. Patch?'

'Socks, it was Socks!'

'That's not American politics, that's American pets. Okay, history. Who was kidnapped by Hector of Troy?'

'Kiki?'

We had to admit this mini pub quiz was pretty one-sided, and went home. I have to say The Husband is a bit of a know-all. He is always pointing out that he got four As at A-level, but as I also frequently point out, when I did my A-levels there was no such thing as course work, and we weren't allowed to take text books or calculators into the exam room. But still The Husband persists in his theory that men are cleverer than women. My feminist cause is not helped by the fact that while watching *The Late Review*, I will comment, 'Hasn't Paul Morley put on weight?'

One of the reasons The Husband thinks my brain only contains facts about Prada and ponies is that I still cannot grasp the niceties of football, no matter how hard I try. My favourite player is, of course, David Beckham, although I couldn't tell you what position he plays. 'At Man United, did he play on the left or the right?' The Husband asked.

'It depends which way they're going,' I replied sagely.

Chapter 43

FEBRUARY 29, 2004
THE INCIDENT WITH THE OVEN GLOVE

For any woman out there who is contemplating proposing to her long-term partner or that nice boy with the twinkly eyes she sees on the train every morning, my advice is, don't!

My vast experience of chasing men shows that it never, ever works. I tried the subtle approach – stalking for two years, buying the house next door – and the rather more direct one, in that I asked a man out (he said no; this was Peanut Butter Mountain Man).

Anyway, I have found out to my extreme disappointment that men are not worth all the effort.

Last week I settled down with Snoopy in front of *The Office*. A few moments later, I heard a yell from downstairs.

'Lizzieeee!' he shouted. I jumped out of my skin, thinking something awful had happened, such as Squeaky pulling a boiling kettle off the hob.

'What?'

'Why did you throw away the oven gloves?' He was really shouting, so I covered Snoopy's ears. He stormed into the room clutching the new, giant cream oven glove I had bought in the Liberty sale. I had thrown the old double ones away because they were frayed and faded. 'What use is this, except for someone with only one arm?' he screamed.

I almost replied that it would be useful if ever Squeaky required eye drops, but instead said calmly, 'Don't ever shout at me like that again.'

'Don't spout that feminist rubbish,' he said. 'If I lose my temper, I shout. If you don't like it, show me the door.'

With that, he disappeared off to bed, and I sat there all alone, watching David Brent, with tears diluting my pasta sauce. I considered sleeping in the spare room, but decided that would only make Susie disorientated.

'If you ever talk to me like that again I will leave,' I had said as a passing shot.

'Oh really, where are you going to go?' he'd replied nastily.

'To my mum's, with Squeaky because the tabbies don't like change.'

I phoned my sister Sue, and she started telling me about a particularly stressful week at work when she had had to go on a course, rush home to pick up her little boy because her partner couldn't, make dinner, combat crumbs, stack the dishwasher and rearrange the laundry that was drying in the living room. I asked whether she missed her life as a single woman, when her drawers were full of ironed knickers, when she had the time to make her own pot pourri, and every episode of *thirtysomething* was videoed, neatly labelled and arranged chronologically. 'Yes, of course,' she said, 'but now Joe is six I can at long last sit down and watch *Pal Joey* on DVD.'

Is that what I have to look forward to if we ever have children: several years without TV? Being single is hugely underrated. Oh for the days when I would get home and everything was as I left it, or when I could choose what film I would see in the cinema, and buy oven gloves with impunity.

'What I need,' I whispered to Snoops, 'is a bit of me time.'

So, I have booked myself in to a retreat in Dorset: no phones, communal vegan dinners, hot basalt and iced marble treatments and shamanic healing. I need to regain my inner calm.

I have become rather concerned, of late, that I am losing my looks. My life has become a lot less glamorous. I used to swan about, hobnobbing with supermodels (an activity that did not involve any type of biscuit), sitting in the front row of couture. And, as part of my role as ambassador for normal women, I felt it my duty to road test as many spa treatments as humanly possible. At places as diverse as Strawberry Hill in Jamaica, the Palace hotel with Leg School atop Capri and the Bliss spa in Manhattan, every extraneous hair was eradicated, the soles of my feet transformed into those of a baby, and I was able to pass the pore-strip challenge.

Now, though – and I blame The Husband for making me feel secure enough to cancel the Aveda block booking and go to the Organic Pub instead – I have reverted to my natural state.

So I am in the retreat, reading *Bergdorf Blondes*, when my mobile rings. I leap on it, fearing I will be evicted. It's him. 'Lizzie, Squeaky is wearing the cat flap again.' I feel dreadfully homesick.

PART FOUR

It all goes horribly wrong

Chapter 44

MARCH 9, 2004
THE ROMANCE, WHERE HAS IT GONE?

'Hi chubs. Found headless chicken in the garden. Snoop was playing with it at the time. Corpse was very downy, very much his type. Thought it might be part of some Hackney ritual, v scared. Asked Mad Chicken Man [his garden backs on to ours] if it was his. He said a fox had massacred his entire coup – nine hens! – and told me to throw it over the fence to him. Having donned a marigold, I missed and threw headless chicken into Sasha's garden next door instead, which upset Sasha v much as he happened to be having a quiet fag. Went and retrieved headless chicken and handed it to visibly revolted road sweeper. What a morning! xx'

Half an hour later, another email arrived...

'Have got biscuits for Susie (kitten) and Squeaky (reducing). Am feeding Susie salmon pâté, which she loves. Haven't booked train, as don't have credit card – can you do it on Internet? Bunmi not at all well. She can't stop coughing. V nauseous and uncommunicative. Will see her when the chemo has worn off a little. Love u chubby chubs, what time will you be getting home for supper?'

Chapter 45

MARCH 14, 2004
JOE COMES TO STAY

My sister Sue and her six-year-old son, Joe, came to stay last
weekend. When they had gone, I was so tired I could no
longer form words, and could only lie supine on the sofa.

Even though they stayed for two nights only, they brought a suitcase, a hold-all, a Playstation2, a Gameboy Advance, a selection of
Playstation games, and a carrier bag full of Joe's special food. He is
a lovely little boy, really chatty, and always wipes his fingers and
uses a plate, but he had this imaginary *Lord of the Rings* sword he
kept wielding and the frantic arm-waving frightened Susie.

When they had gone, The Husband shut the door and said,
'You'd make an appalling mum.'

I considered arguing my case for a few seconds, but what would
be the point? 'I know. I wish I was more nurturing and cuddly with
children, but I can't do it. They have so many colourful possessions
made of non-environmentally sound materials, they walk around
with glasses of stuff and you have to keep giving them meals, which
they then don't eat.'

I am the youngest of seven: Clare, resembles Patsy in *Absolutely
Fabulous*; Philip, lawyer; Nick, seventies throwback; Lynnie, lives
in Sydney, still hasn't motivated herself to get a pair of glasses
despite being almost blind; Tony, moved to Edinburgh because of
the licensing laws; Sue, we know, is a nurse; then me, the Baby.
People think it was the resultant chaos that must have put me off.
But it wasn't chaotic at all: my mum ensured our clothes were
ironed, the floors polished, and we never once ate a shop-bought

sponge. But it did all look too exhausting. I never once saw my mother put her feet up and read a book, or take a bath that lasted more than five minutes. I vowed that would never happen to me: ironing when I should be watching *ER*.

The Husband, on the other hand, had rather enjoyed his week-end with Joe, having someone to play football with. They even wore identical outfits: outsize combats, hooded sweat tops and brightly coloured, enormously soled trainers.

'And I don't think bringing a child in to the world is very environmentally friendly,' I continued. 'Look at all the disposable nappy mountains.'

He rolled his eyes. 'What you mean to say is, you don't want to go through childbirth.' I agree that going through labour at my age would be terribly ageing: all those free radicals from straining would be flying around.

But then, within a few days of each other, two of my girlfriends had babies. First, India had a baby daughter, a dark little doppel-ganger with starfish fingers. Then Michelle had twins, which I am sure came as something of a relief, as at one point she had measured five feet around the waist and began to despair of ever going into Topshop again. I saw the way their boyfriends looked at them, all proud and misty.

'You are never going to look at me that way,' I said to The Husband on the way home from the hospital.

'I know,' he said, turning to look at me. 'Let's compromise. Why don't we adopt?

LISTS FOR AND AGAINST ADOPTING

Against:

   1. I would have to take time off work (or maybe this is a for?).

   2. Squeaky would get jealous.

   3. I would have to turn the minimalist office into a nursery, installing brightly coloured mobile and patterned wallpaper, or risk the baby being unable to focus well into her teens.

   4. I wouldn't be able to lie in until noon at weekends, and then watch TV in bed with a hot liquid.

   5. I'd have to go to Sainsbury's ALL THE TIME.

   6. Snoopy would no longer be able to sit on the bread board.

   7. We wouldn't be able to eat out three nights a week or, in fact, ever.

   8. I'd turn into one of those women who bang on about their child's IQ/school fees/ horrible diseases/ the MMR jab/the logistics of the school run.

   9. The house would smell of Johnson's Baby Powder.

   10. I'd have to buy a bigger dishwasher and buy those awful primary colour plastic spoons and a plastic bib with a trough.

   11. The kitchen floor is limestone, and would probably cause head injuries.

For:

   1. I would be able to buy lots of sweet mini designer clothes, and snuggly blankets and tiny teddies.

   2. I would, at last, have something in common with Kate Moss.

   3. I'd be able to turn up at friends' parties for their offspring and not feel inadequate and lazy.

   4. I already have a house-husband, although what would happen

during *Eurogoals* is anyone's guess.

5. Christmas would be more fun.

6. I would have to learn how to cook.

7. Maybe The Husband would think there is more point to us being together. He isn't talking to me much at the moment; his office emits only eerie silence and cabbagey smells.

8. We would give a child a lovely home and pets. We would take someone out of poverty, a life where she might become a cleaner, or starve, and give her nice things and a future and love.

I showed The Husband the list. 'Well,' he said, 'if you had made a list of for and against adopting Susie, we would never have got her. We had to keep her indoors for a year because she was so wild, which meant having cat litter in the house. And she scratched the £4,000 Matthew Hilton sofa, which went all bobbly, and made puncture wounds in your Eames, and all you said was, "Awwww, she's so sweet." And the other day I gave Squeaky an inoffensive and affectionate tap on her head and you shouted, "Don't tap my cats!!" and threatened to change the locks, saying you wouldn't leave me here during the day.'

Chapter 46

APRIL 4, 2004
I GET HOME FROM THE OSCARS TO FIND SQUEAKY HAS RUN OUT OF HER SPECIAL BISCUITS

I have just returned from three days in Los Angeles, where I had to file a report on the Oscar parties. All very glamorous, but it meant 22 hours in Economy, and not much food (there are no carbs to be found in California, not a one), and I was depressed because I had just spent many hours standing in line next to Scarlett Johansson. I had lots of phone calls from The Husband saying he missed me and that the cats were all present and correct. He mentioned the builder had been in to paint the kitchen. I felt panic rising in my chest but suppressed it.

I arrived home Tuesday lunchtime, feeling grubby and blocked-arteried, and found the following:

1. No hot water.

2. Squeaky had run out of her special biscuits.

3. The kitchen sink hadn't been Ciffed, the dishwasher and limestone floor were covered in paint flecks ('Did he use a brush or did he USE A ROLLER?'), the washing hadn't been done meaning I faced a huge backlog, and my shirt wasn't ironed for work the next day.

4. There was no food in the fridge, despite the fact I left him £120 to buy nice groceries. He says he 'ate out'.

5. There was a pile of bills next to the front door. Why doesn't he ever pick them up? Does he only have periphery vision? Can he not bend, despite the hours he spends every day kick boxing?

'Didn't you think it would be nice if I came home to a tidy house and some food, having worked all weekend?' I asked him. He smirked. I know he doesn't consider what I do work, just because I don't write about the EU. 'Are you going to get Squeaky's biscuits?'

'I'll pop out later,' he said, sitting at his G4 laptop with its wireless Internet. He thinks sitting in front of his computer is some sort of defence. 'What is the point cleaning up when H comes on Friday?' I pointed out that was still three days away.

'Are you going to clean the floor?'

'No. I really don't want to,' he said, tap tap tapping away with a look on his face that said, I'm concentrating on real work you stupid female. 'By the way, I like the haircut.'

While I had been in LA, as well as visiting the hotel's eyebrow station, I had had my hair done for the Oscars by Nicky Clarke, celebrity hairdresser to the stars. It was still long, but with expert choppy layers. Nicky kindly informed me that I had, all my life, been parting it on the wrong side. I asked him what was the most common mistake women make with their hair. 'Not changing their style once they hit forty,' he said ominously.

'You really like it?' I asked The Husband, thinking I might forgive him.

'Yeah, it makes you look slightly less mad. It was like a helmet before; you looked like Ozzy Osbourne, only without the round glasses.'

Chapter 47

APRIL 18, 2004
THE DENOUEMENT

I have found out why he has been so quiet and uncommunicative these past few weeks. I was upstairs, lying on the bed watching the penultimate episode of *Sex and the City*, when he came in to the room, turned the TV off, and lay down next to me. He was upset. I thought initially it was because he had been talking to Bunmi for most of the afternoon. We talked about that for a bit and then, with emotion filling his throat, he said, 'Lizzie, I really need to be a dad.'

I sat up. What does he mean? Why is he saying this in such a strange manner...didn't we talk about adopting one day? He wants to leave me and go out with someone younger, what?

'I want to stop thinking about myself. I'm thirty now. I don't care about being successful any more; I just want to bring up a child. I think I'd make a really good dad.'

'Have a child with me, or with someone else?' I asked bravely.

'Well, you don't really want a kid, do you? Not really. And I can't do that.'

I went cold. 'No, I thought you didn't want one. You are always going on about how your friends say women change when they have a baby, and that it can ruin a relationship. Of course I want one.' I don't know if I meant what I said. All I knew was that it wasn't about adoption. He wanted to leave me. This was just an excuse.

'I am so relieved,' he said finally. 'I was telling Bunmi that I wanted a baby and you didn't, and she kept saying I had to talk to you, but I kept putting it off. She said I'd be sacrificing the fact I have a lovely wife who cares about me. And the night you went to LA I came to bed, and I could hear the baby next door crying, and it didn't annoy me one bit.'

We started to get quite excited. He said he would get a job, tomorrow; he doesn't care what he does as long as he can bring in some money, and would surf the Internet to find out how we go about it. 'How about adopting from India?' he asked, propping himself up on a pillow. 'As I'm Punjabi it shouldn't be a problem. A little girl?'

He told me I would have to put carpet in the spare room. Oh no; my oak floor's the colour of Calvin Klein's floor in the Hamptons.

He fell asleep, and I just sat there, thinking. I was confused. Yes, I do want to have a child with him, I am just scared and apprehensive and keen to do a good job. I know I would never shout at a child, unless it was about to run under a lorry or set fire to Squeaky, and that I would love it and be patient and give it all the things I never had, like a pony and advice about tampons. Even though he had said, 'I can't think of anyone I would rather have a child with', I know in my bones that, if I had said no, he would have left me. Just like that. What if I had had cancer and chemo and was infertile, or had polycystic ovaries, would he just leave me? I wouldn't leave him if he had no sperm. It's like the last line in my favourite film, *Some Like It Hot* (which I took him to see at the National Film Theatre and he didn't appreciate one bit). 'Nobody's perfect.'

Chapter 48

APRIL 25, 2004
WE VISIT THE TWINS

This is what I have done so far in our quest to adopt. Because we have to be vetted before we can adopt abroad, I phoned Hackney social services and left several messages, and sent an email. No reply. I have also emailed an agency in Calcutta to get in contact with the Mother Teresa orphanage, although The Husband said the child would then speak Bengali, whereas he speaks Punjabi and 'it would be nice to be able to chat to it'.

I think he will make a good dad, even though the novel writing, despite the new laptop, has ground to a halt and he hasn't done anything about getting a job. But I can't think of any other man who would, in the course of the average day looking after Susie...

1. Poach cod and blow on it.

2. Trail after her with the aforementioned fish.

3. Never close the door to his office in case she wants to pop in.

4. Sleep like a long dead starfish to accommodate a puss in each angle.

5. Be prepared to stop every conversation mid-flow whenever I say, 'Look at Susie!'

6 Stay with her while she eats in case Squeaky waddles over.

7. Never smoke, even in the garden.

I suggested we go and visit Michelle and her twins. I thought it would give him some idea of what to expect in the way of mess and chaos. How tidy would the flat be? How much would Michelle be missing her job on *Glamour*? Would there be stains? Has she bricked off the door to the roof terrace and given away her Manolo Blahniks?

'Yeah, well, you can stay and chat to Michelle while I take Jamie down the pub,' he said.

'No, no, no. You have to put yourself in Jamie's place, and imagine your life too. You won't be able to just stare at the TV and leave hot liquids on the floor.'

We drove over one Saturday afternoon (she is too tired for visitors after 5 p.m.) and the girls are gorgeous, very naughty, and Michelle seems happy. Jamie has risen to the challenge, and has become very proactive and started to use his initiative and buy semi-skimmed milk when it runs out rather than just leave the empty carton in the fridge. I tried to sit down but everywhere was full up. Michelle did look tired, though.

'Why don't you have one of those amazing non-invasive face lifts,' I suggested, 'with muscular suggestion together with hypnotic words to give you an open, smooth expression. Shall I give you the number? It only takes 45 minutes.'

She gave me a look that told me I had, finally, gone completely mad.

Chapter 49

MAY 2, 2004
I AM NOT GOING TO SCUPPER THINGS
BY BEING NEGATIVE

O h, I don't know. One minute we're up, the next we're down. At least when you are single you potter off home after work, open your little tub of M&S tomato and mascarpone sauce, boil the pasta, make one plate dirty, sit in front of the TV with the puss and there you have it: quite a nice, cosy evening. It might be a bit tidy and predictable, but at least it's not a stomach-churning roller-coaster ride.

Ever since The Husband said those words, 'I need to be a dad,' in that deadpan, final way, I have been wondering. It turns out he had been mulling the subject of children over in his head for weeks, without saying a word to me. He had been talking it over with Bunmi. He has been spending so much time with her recently, driving her to St Barts, picking her up, buying her noodles and reading to her. When I told him I might be jealous of the fact they spend so much time together (when I am chained to my desk for what seems like every waking moment just so that he can 'work out what I want to do with my life' and 'finish my novel' and spend time with Bunmi) he jumped down my throat, and said, 'Jealous that you haven't got terminal cancer?' Which wasn't what I meant at all. I do think that night during *Sex and the City* he was going to announce he was leaving me. He didn't expect old miss fussy pants with her organised drawers and ironed tea towels to say yes to a baby. After three years together, during which time he has contributed nary a chocolate biscuit or a dishcloth to the household, I feel well and truly miffed.

When I asked why he didn't talk to me about it, he replied dramatically, 'There are a lot of silences in our relationship.' Hmmm.

But I have to say that since these moments of doubt, we have been on more of an even keel, with something to look forward to (e.g. a new person arriving) rather than just basking in our usual round of organic dinners, trips to the movies and new purchases from the Conran Shop (I have just bought a Nigella Lawson salt pig; fabulous). I have decided I am not going to do what I usually do, i.e. scupper things with my intense negativity ('He says he wants to bring up a child with me, but does that still mean he will be there when I get home?' – that sort of thing). I am always worrying, and can tend towards clinginess. The other day, he shuffled off to Hackney Town Hall to renew his resident's parking permit for another year (I bought him an old Golf; my nerves couldn't take him driving my BMW), and the thought shot unbidden through my head, 'Oh, goody. That means he's still going to be here at Christmas.'

Aren't I mad? Aren't women, generally, a bit bonkers when it comes to relationships?

I went round to see Jeremy's new loft. He is living in blissful singledom, ordering those obscure cleaning products on the Internet, arranging his books according to the colour of their spines. He asked me how we were getting on. Jerry has been there for me during the wilderness years, the crazy six months with Mad Richard, and this time he said, 'Lizzie, you can be really annoying. You are a bit of a pessimist. You have to get over the fact that you didn't win best garden in a saucer when you were seven. [I dropped it, but my mum told me it was still lovely and that I should still enter. Other children had turf, mirrors for ponds, fruit made out of marzipan, bonsai trees, miniature wheelbarrows; I had a plate of soil. I didn't even get Highly Commended. I have never trusted my mum's advice since.] It's about time something went right for you. Lighten up. You will be a lovely mummy. Your husband loves you. Sometimes he might have doubts, but so do you. That's how life is.'

Chapter 50

MAY 9, 2004
WE MEET MARIE

I got up on Saturday afternoon and came downstairs to an open jar of instant coffee (I have ground my own Fair Trade beans since the early eighties) on the draining board, a horrid teaspoon and a kettle that had turned black. 'Why is the kettle black?' I asked The Husband, who was reading the papers.

'How should I know. Why don't you just buy a new one?'

Then I opened the door to the cupboard under the stairs and the floor was under several inches of murky water. 'Yeah, that happened yesterday,' he said, not looking up.

'Why didn't you mop it up?' I asked.

'No point.'

I sat at the table. As he had gone quiet, I asked him what was wrong.

'It's Saturday, and the minute you get up you go on a cleaning fit,' he said. 'Complaining about a bit of water. What about if we get a child? Things won't be perfect then. They mess things up. They do things like put sandwiches in the video recorder. I won't be doing housework then, you know, not if it means time away from watching TV with it, or reading to it.'

I think that was a bit unkind. I almost venture that having a baby would mean more housework, not less.

On Wednesday evening, for which I hared home early at top speed in case she thought I was too career-orientated, we had our first visit from our social worker. She is called Marie. In preparation the limestone floor had been professionally cleaned, the lawn was re-turfed and I had undergone the muscle suggestion facial the day before so that I looked relaxed. When I got home I threw hot soapy water down the front steps. All day, hubby was banned from making a sandwich. She arrived at 6.30 p.m. and we sat in the sitting room.

She explained the adoption process to us. She would visit us six or seven times on a weekly basis, finding out about our childhoods, our careers, our relationship. 'We have a loving, stable relationship,' The Husband said, and I swelled with pride and affection for him. She said she also needed to interview three people who know us as a couple. We nominated Kerry, Jeremy and Paula, Bunmi's girlfriend, as she is already a mum. (When I told Jeremy that he would have to be interviewed, he said, 'Shall I leave out Mad Richard? And the fact you have an obsessive–compulsive disorder?')

The process should take about five months, and as we are adopting abroad the fee would be £3000. Marie then asked me why I had never had children. I mumbled something about never having found the right man, which is true. (What I didn't tell her is that

I never thought my body had an ability to function properly. I didn't start menstruating until I was 19, and then my periods stopped and didn't return until I was about 27; the fact I only ate one Loseley Hazelnut yoghurt a day might have had something to do with it. Then there was the non-sex while skiing incident. And it wasn't just the garden in a saucer; everything I did went wrong. In PE, I could only ever manage a forward roll, and even that hurt. When I was supposed to hurdle, I always refused. Although I loved horses, I was never a confident rider; they would always walk me into a patch of nettles and then put their heads down and chew. That I could actually make a person and it would turn out okay was, I always thought, an impossibility.)

Then Squeaky let the side down very badly. She had been sitting between me and Marie, following the conversation, and then, unprovoked, she lunged at Marie and bit her hand. She actually drew blood. 'She is very good with children,' I lied as I showed Marie to the front door.

'Just think,' I said to The Husband after she had gone. 'Our baby has probably already been born. She is sitting somewhere, all straight backed and patient, waiting for us to go and get her.'

'You're going to have to get rid of Squeaky,' he said. And I'm still not sure if he was joking.

Chapter 51

MAY 23, 2004

HE ADMITS THAT, WITH ACCESS TO A MINI BAR,
HE WOULD HAVE EXTRAMARITAL SEX

I must remember never to ask his opinion on anything. Women lie to keep men's egos inflated. Even when he tipped the scales at almost 18 stone, I still told him he wasn't fat and was much more handsome than David Beckham. We have just watched Real Madrid being beaten three nil. 'Poor David,' I say. 'I don't think his mind is on the game.'

'Poor David nothing. I'm glad he's been caught with his pants down. Tears in his eyes on *Parkinson* when he heard Posh sing, my arse. It proves New Man never existed. Believe me, all men, given money and time on their own in a hotel, would happily accept the offer of extramarital sex.'

'What do you mean, all men? But he loves Victoria and his boys…'

'That has got nothing to do with it. He doesn't want a divorce, just some extra-curricular nooky, someone to stroke his ego, who doesn't ask him to move his SUV or change his walk-in wardrobe from spring/summer to autumn/winter.'

'Okay then, bearing in mind you stand to lose custody of all of your fur babies, would you have sex with a woman if you were away somewhere with access to a minibar and you thought I wouldn't find out?'

'Of course I would. I'm a man, aren't I?'

The next day, I email David, The Husband's best friend (and someone whom I regard as a boyfriend back-up).

'All men need a shed, somewhere they can go to think, mend things, wank. As long as you give him that he'll be fine.'

Mend things? Now that would be useful.

Chapter 52

MAY 30, 2004
I THREATEN TO BAKE A VICTORIA SPONGE

This Thursday will mark the four-year anniversary of our first date. I asked The Husband how he would be marking the event. 'Emine's boyfriend sent her a huge bunch of tulips to mark their two-year anniversary,' I told him. 'And he took her out to dinner, having booked the restaurant himself!'

'We could watch Newcastle in the UEFA cup semi-final,' he said, in all seriousness. 'I can't send you flowers because I haven't got any money. I could pick some,' he added, looking through the kitchen window. (I have just had the garden done, at huge expense. I told the very nice gardener called Jeremy that he couldn't kill the snails, but had to re-home them, which he did; they now live happily on London Fields. I have also confiscated The Husband's football.)

Apparently, money is the most common cause of conflict among couples, and it is also starting to become a bit of an issue with us, coming a close second to the rogue socks and piles of coppers problem. The Husband seems to be under the impression he doesn't cost very much, just because he rotates two outsize M&S T-shirts and doesn't use Revive moisturiser and eye cream.

Because The Husband came straight to live with me from his

mum's, he has no idea how expensive everything is. Take, for example, our last phone bill, which was £800. Bear in mind that I am not at home during the day and only use the phone at weekends, when it is free. One mobile number kept appearing, over and over again, on our latest bill, with numerous text messages and four-hour conversations, so (naughty, I know, but you can't be sure any more, not post-Beckham), I rang it. An answerphone kicked in, and it turned out to be David.

'What on earth do you talk to David about all day?' I asked when I got home from work. 'I could have gone on an exotic holiday for the price of the phone bill....'

'Well, he told me yesterday that his girlfriend makes him pay half of everything – groceries, the gas bill – and if he hasn't got the money, she runs a tab. Can you believe that?'

'Why shouldn't he pay half?' I asked, incredulous.

'She earns more than he does,' he replied, pulling open a pillow of lamb's lettuce, which he proceeded to drown in olive oil that costs £14.99 a bottle.

'No, that's not fair,' I said. 'He should pay his way, and so should you. You're like an extra giant pet. What if I decided I wanted to downsize when we get a baby? I might get all broody and want to spend my time cooking Victoria sponges. Think of all the organic nappies we are going to have to buy.'

He began to look very worried indeed.

JUNE 6, 2004
THINGS ARE STILL VERY UNBALANCED

He is on a bit of a slippery slope at the moment. Having got in to shape last summer, he managed to put on a stone during winter, mainly by eating chocolate digestives before going to bed. I think part of the problem is that he is at home all day doing very little. I decided to email him some tasks:

1. Get a new mini light bulb for the Swedish light in the kitchen.

2. Buy car tax.

3. Mend the light on YOUR car or you will be arrested.

4. Do the supermarket shopping on line with Ocado, bearing in mind you mustn't go off-list.

5. Feed Susan.

6. Mend the tumble dryer.

7. Water the garden.

When I got home, he hadn't done a single one of these things, not even the easy ones. Susie was looking very hungry, and he had draped the laundry around the house. He was very lucky it had rained. Now, I could do what my sister Sue does after a hard day's nursing when she gets home to find the house in chaos, and take an early oily bath, but I just couldn't let it go.

'Why is the bed unmade? And why haven't you changed the light bulb or fed Sue? You are so mean. If I had been home all day not writing my novel I would have tidied and lit candles and made a rhubarb crumble. It's not fair. What have you been doing all day?'

'I finished reading my book. *My Traitor's Heart* by Rian Malan — very good. I felt really tired for some reason. I think I am not eating enough.'

I told him he was really annoying.

'Well, you annoy me,' he said.

'How?'

'I can't stand the way that, whenever we are watching a film, you can never comprehend what is going on. "Which cop? Who was murdered?" How did you ever grasp *Dirty Dancing* on your own? And the way you only ever open the fridge using the bottom of your T-shirt. And that you are always throwing my things away. Where did my toothbrush go, by the way? Why are the windows always open? And it annoys me that whenever you get me a glass of water, you only fill it halfway. What is that all about?'

'It's so you don't spill.'

'What am I, a toddler?!'

I have been trying to loosen up, I promise. Towels can, on occasion, be used twice. Sofa cushions can be left unplumped, but only if you are returning within twenty minutes. The overhead light can be put on, but only if someone is sewing or bathing a wound or administering eye drops; reading doesn't count.

I only got his reply to my email of tasks the next day.

'Chubby! Will do as told. How do I water garden? I've been having a competition with the cats to see who has the best tail. I have £20 in my Post Office account; £45 in total. Hurrah! Enough for me to get steaming drunk with David and get the night bus home.'

I seriously think he either has to finish his novel, or get a job.

Chapter 53

JUNE 13, 2004
DOES BRAD PITT TAKE THE RUBBISH OUT?

On Wednesday evening, we had our third visit from Marie. This time, she asked us how we would bring up the child to be proud of its own culture, how we would cope with a child who might be unable to 'attach' to us, and how we would tell her that she was adopted. Her questions made me think very hard about what we were about to embark on. The baby might have behavioural problems, there might be nothing to tell us who her natural parents were, she might have been abused, or be sick. We would have to help her deal with the fact that she was abandoned. Then Marie asked us what would happen if our marriage broke down. We looked at each other.

'Well,' The Husband said, shifting in his seat. 'It's your house, so you would stay here with the baby. But we would share equal custody.'

'It's not my house,' I said, panicking. 'We are married, so we own half each. What do you mean I would stay here with the baby? Where are you going? Who would keep Snoopy?'

Obviously, it would be best for Baby if we never split up, but if it can happen to Brad and Jen... (he said early on in an interview: 'Let's see where this thing is going...I'm not sure if it really is in our nature to be with someone for the rest of our lives'; I wonder if he took the rubbish out and paired his socks?) ...then even the perfect couple for whom everything matches, from the honey-coloured hair to the number of zeros in their bank accounts, has to think very seriously about the possibility of not always being together. Of course, we are the couple for whom absolutely nothing matches. He is worrying about his student loan; I am worrying about breaking a hip and catching shingles. I do wonder whether, if he had opted for a 24-year-old with a PhD in economics, he would have had a simpler, happier life. He wouldn't, for example, be answering probing questions once a week about his attitude towards smacking (never), and nannies (again, never; I knew my cat sitter for four years before I left Snoopy alone with him, and even then I insisted on daily faxed updates).

Over the next two weeks, Marie will interview us separately to find out more. I am getting really excited. I think Marie likes us. I think it will all work out for a change.

Then, in bed that night, snuggling, while I was stroking his back, The Husband asked me, 'Are you sure you are not too old and tired to bring up a child?'

I was miffed, to put it mildly. Who, I said, has risen at 6 a.m. for the past four years without fail so as not to be late for work, who has rarely got home before 8 p.m., who has worked numerous Sundays and Bank Holidays, and has brought up a feral kitten who to this day wakes me three or four times in the night for her biscuits while he just lies there, oblivious to the world, like a dead person? 'And,' I continued, 'who doesn't take regular naps, and moan when the rubbish has to be taken out.' But he was already snoring.

Chapter 54

JUNE 20, 2004
I MUST REMEMBER I AM NOT HIS MUMMY

1. When he went to a pub quiz in Soho, bearing in mind he has lived in London all his life, he phoned me at work to ask me if I could look up where he was going on the A to Z.

2. I asked him to please mow the new lawn and, after a long, sunny day, I phoned at six to see how it had gone. 'It looked as though it might rain [he has a perverse fear of rain and will never go to the shops or out to the bin in even a drizzle, although he will happily jog or play football in a rainstorm]. I might have got electrocuted,' he said. Our mower is the sort you push and pull. It doesn't have a plug.

3. He has got into the habit of saying, 'Can you do it, Lizzie?' about ABSOLUTELY EVERYTHING. And because he is so hopeless at mending things ('Where do we keep the screwdriver?') or phoning up people to complain (I once persuaded him to phone British Gas and berate them about a huge mistake on the bill, and all I could hear were the words, 'No, that doesn't matter, thanks a lot, bye, bye'), I just give up and take over. Why isn't he more like my dad? Whenever we went anywhere as a family he would drive and my mum would sit in the front, buttering rolls. The first time my mum ever had to use a Switch card or write a cheque was after he died (she got quite excited in Waitrose when they asked her how much cashback she wanted, 'Oooh, £100?' and was disappointed when they told her she could only have £50). Whenever The Husband and I go out I have to drive because he is 'scared of dual carriageways'.

I told Emine. She said I have to cut the apron strings and shove him out into the big, wide world. 'He managed to do things before he met me,' I wailed. 'He had a job, a bus pass.'

'If my boyfriend phoned me while I was at work in a high-pressure job to ask for directions, I'd be furious,' she said (but then she does have a beautiful face, Gisele's hair, extreme youth). 'You are incredibly patient, but you have to remember you are not his mummy.'

The other day we were in the car and, while I was driving, The Husband was texting furiously. 'Who are you texting?' I asked, cross to be left out.

'David.' (David is in the process of splitting up with Danielle; she wants a baby, he is one.)

'Has he moved out yet?'

'No, I told him not to until he is back on his feet. He is on a cushy number there, so why not?'

'But that's not fair,' I said. 'She might not want to waste time, she might want to start finding a replacement boyfriend.'

'He's my friend. I told him what was best for him, not her.'

Later that night in bed, I asked him, 'Do you love me unconditionally? Do you pine for me to get home and feed you and play with your ears?'

'Mmmm,' he said, turning on his back so I could rub his tummy.

I have confirmed my suspicions. After thirty years of feminism, men have, finally, mutated into giant pets.

Chapter 55

SUSAN IS MISSING

Oh God, oh God, oh God. Susan is missing. I saw her on Friday night, when she shot into the house as a police helicopter buzzed the garden. I didn't see her all day Saturday, and was really worried, and kept calling her, but in the middle of the night she woke me up to ask for her prawns. I then left on Sunday to go to the Cannes film festival (ghastly; I got caught up in Uma Thurman's wake on the red carpet, and when she stopped to be interviewed by the E! channel I had to walk on, stupidly, by myself), and when I got back on Monday, The Husband hadn't seen her at all. We spent the evening calling until we were both hoarse. Nothing. Normally, I will go into the garden, call 'Susie darling!' and you will hear a little cry and a rustling of the undergrowth and then a crash as she lands on the fence. Then she will drop, as slowly and softly as if by parachute, into the middle of the lawn, motor round for a bit, and then skid to a halt for a head rub. She will then tiptoe after me in to the house, where I will have her supper waiting for her under the spare bed. She is still painfully shy and skittish; The Husband is under strict instructions never to sneeze in the house. In summer, she loves to be outside, climbing in trees and sunbathing in flowerpots, but she has never gone far before.

I sent an email to Celia Hammond, asking her advice. She thought Sue would be able to feed herself, and that she wouldn't have gone far. She told me about a friend who had also adopted a feral, and when his cat disappeared he slept by his back door for several days, waiting with biscuits. Celia advised me to leaflet the neighbourhood, so last night I set off, armed with 200 copies of the following:

LOST

Small female brown tabby cat, black stripes with a black tip
to her tail. Answers to the name of Susie. Very shy and
easily frightened. Missing since Saturday night. Please
check outbuildings, basements and sheds.
REWARD. Please call…

When I got home, he was standing in the garden with a huge
G&T and a cigarette. 'I can't stand this, the not knowing,' he said.
'Isn't it always the way that when you love someone, they always
end up hurting you? If we get a baby, won't that mean 18 years of
feeling like this?'

I tried to reassure him that Snoop had once gone missing and I
had been wild with grief, but that he had turned up again, exactly
two weeks later (it was as if he had gone on a package holiday). He
was tired and dirty and thin, but he was safe. (Squeaky, chubby little madam that she is, has, obviously, never gone further than the
flowerbed by the back door.) So, that night, on Tuesday, we walked
the streets, knocking on doors, putting leaflets in letterboxes. A
great many people do not hose their wheelie bins. The Husband
went to bed at nine because he couldn't stand being awake. He said
it was like when Spurs lost the FA Cup Final, only much, much
worse. I sat in the garden in the dark, picturing her little face, her
stripy body (she always looks as if she is wearing pyjamas), and
remembering how she would jump into bed with me the moment I
put the light out, manoeuvre her tiny rump with a shove, before
sleeping soundly, one paw outstretched in a black power salute. She
is the sweetest, gentlest little cat. I hope she isn't trapped some-

where. Or run over. Or savaged by foxes. Please come home, sweetheart. I can't bear it without you.

JULY 4, 2004
SHE IS STILL MISSING

We are supposed to be going on holiday to Mauritius. It is to be a second honeymoon, since the first one was such a disaster. Exactly one week later, and we still haven't found Susie. I have leafleted over 250 houses, some of the inhabitants of which were really rather rude, and spent every night roaming the streets, shining a torch, rattling biscuits, calling, calling, calling. We have had two sightings by neighbours, but when we turned up, cat basket and prawns to hand, there was no sign.

The Husband says she has simply decided she wants her freedom, but that is ridiculous. She already has her freedom – she can pop out of the cat flap, climb trees, doesn't have to sit on laps or suffer the indignity of being picked up – but she also has her special cushion, and head rubs, and M&S food. I am going to keep looking, but as each day goes by I have the awful feeling she will no longer recognise her name, or be able to picture my face. Her absence has made me very emotional, so that at the slightest provocation – an episode of *ER*, say, or the lights turning red – I burst into tears.

The most annoying thing is that next weekend we are supposed to be going away, but how can we when she is still missing? We really need this break. When we get a baby we will be consigned to places with bunk beds and novelty water chutes. In preparation for having to wear my Burberry bikini, I have been Power House Eating (invented by health and beauty guru Leslie Kenton; I used to work with her on *Mirabella*. She wore only black in winter, white in summer, and ate her own placenta). Basically, I have lots of things sprouting on the windowsills in an attempt to banish cellulite. The time from soil to mouth, apparently, is all important. I phoned him.

'I really want to go,' The Husband said callously. 'I could do with a bit of snorkelling. Do you want moonlit dinners on the beach, far away from free radicals, or do you want to spend the week rigid in bed, listening out for that little shout saying she is back and wants her bowl. It's totally up to you.'

Chapter 56

I READ ELLE DECO, HE READS THE HUMAN STAIN

I brought up the flirting star I had interviewed because The Husband has been going on and on about how attractive he is to other women. He is a bit of a crosspatch at the moment. I think the reasons are threefold:

1. We still haven't found Susie. I won't go on about this; suffice to say, a light has gone out in my life.

2. We weren't able to go on our second honeymoon.

3. We have reached a hiatus on the baby adoption front. We have completed our interviews, and now have to wait while our friends are interrogated; we will go before the adoption panel in September. I am tempted to start buying Bill Amberg papooses and delicious organic cotton smocks from Babylist but feel that would be tempting fate; plus we have no idea what size she will be.

We were lying in bed last night – I was reading *Elle Decoration*, he was reading *The Human Stain* – when I started to tell him about the sexy star, and that I thought he had fancied me. 'In your dreams,' The Husband said, turning over and alarming Squeaky. 'Didn't you tell him you are old enough to be his mother?'

That was rather harsh. I only brought up the star because in the Organic Pub earlier in the week, he had made a point of saying how beautiful the Chinese waitress was, and how obvious it was she fancied him. 'Well, go out with her then,' I had said. 'Take your £2.50 and show her a good time.'

He went out on the town with David a couple of nights ago, and came home a different boy. David is a bad influence at the moment, having just left Danielle. I asked whether she was upset. 'Yes, there was all the usual stuff: tears, offers to support him for a year. But you know what, I really admire David. He doesn't suffer any guilt. He doesn't ever believe he owes anyone anything.'

I nearly said, 'What, not even a couple of years' worth of grocery bills on some mythical tab?' but didn't bother.

Anyway, then he said, 'Have we paid for the adoption thing yet?'

'Well, no, they haven't sent a bill. And if they had I would have told you, because we agreed we were each going to pay half. You said you were going to get a job, even a part-time one in a bar [although not at the Organic Pub, obviously], because what was important to you was raising a child. You no longer wanted to gad around aimlessly.'

'Hmmm. I have been thinking this is all too soon for me. Maybe I am still too young to go through this malarkey. David was saying he is going to bum around South America for a bit this summer and that maybe I should go with him. It depends how Bunmi is, of course.'

JULY 18, 2004
I REVEAL THAT DAVID HAS OFFERED BACK-UP

You see! I am not the only woman to have a lazy husband! A new survey has just been published which states, more than thirty years after *Cosmopolitan* told us we could have it all, that, well, we can't. Nine out of ten women said that they still do the bulk of the household chores, while 81 per cent of mothers said they have to take time off work if their child is sick, rather than the father, even if they earn more. I phoned The Husband (I was at work, of course; he was at home sitting on the new iron garden seat holding the hosepipe. I had asked him to dead head the geraniums, and he looked at me as if I was completely barmy) and read out the statistics to him.

'That's how it should be,' he said. 'You are better at cleaning and organising.'

I asked my colleague, Grant, whether or not he shares the chores with his wife. 'Of course!' he said indignantly. 'I take the children out at weekends, I cook, I make the packed lunches for school, I look after the car, pay the bills, book the gîte…'

I phoned The Husband back and told him. 'See, Grant is in the office almost as much as I am and he does tasks.'

'Well, so do I,' he protested. 'I do the washing and monitor the cats and order DVDs on Amazon and today I ordered twenty cans of Stella through Ocado.' What about my black organic grapes? 'Ummm.'

Give a man a shopping list and a credit card and he will forget half of the things on the list and you will end up having to go shopping in your lunch hour. And he might think he does a lot of housework, but he doesn't. He doesn't empty the swing bin; he doesn't lubricate the steel surfaces before he goes to bed; he doesn't clean the cat flap.

Anyway, after the bombshell that he might be going to South America for a bit, that night in bed he offered to plump my pillows and give me a bed bath. Ha bloody ha. I was so annoyed I told him that, a few months after we started going out, David phoned me to say that, if I ever dumped the feckless boyfriend, to bear him in mind. 'Thanks for telling me,' The Husband said, looking down through his eyelashes. 'I am not angry at either of you. It is just good to know he did that.'

I know I was mean, but so were his deliberate attempts to undermine my confidence. David is finding life without Danielle quite hard. He is living with Dr Paul and, to be quite frank, their house now smells of boy. 'Do you want to go back to life before you met me?' I asked The Husband. 'When your duvet never even had a cover?'

Chapter 57

JULY 25, 2004
SUSIE IS RETURNED TO THE FOLD

What a weird and wonderful week. On Wednesday, while he was out, I watched *Cold Mountain* on DVD and, feeling really teary, went out into the garden at 11 p.m. to call Susie. I thought I heard a strange little barking mew but couldn't work out where it was coming from, and then it stopped. I told The Husband when he got home, and he said that if it had been Sue, why hadn't she come when I called? And that if she was locked in somewhere, she wouldn't have survived nearly four weeks without water. While I was at work the next day, he went out looking for her and discovered, while chatting to a neighbour, that the old Chicken Man had died a few weeks ago, and his house was empty.

We immediately thought that Susie must be locked in his house, maybe with access to a tap. So The Husband searched Chicken Man's garden, and in doing so came across a locked shed, which he opened, to discover half a dozen chickens, most of whom had already died. He fetched water and muesli, which kept the survivors going until the RSPCA arrived. But still no Susie.

On Friday evening, after dinner at the Organic Pub, I was so fired up and determined to find her that I went in to the garden at midnight and started calling and listening. And again, I heard mewing, louder this time, and the little old lady who lives two gardens down heard too, and she started calling as well. I yelled for The Husband, who had gone to sleep on the sofa (after his feast of organic salmon, olive-oil mash and braised fennel), and he came out and heard her too. After much scouting and shouting, we decided the noise could only be coming from the Wendy House next door. The family had gone on holiday, so we couldn't ask them to let us have a look; so, having grabbed the step ladder, I climbed over the fence, ignoring the rose thorns, behaving quite as if I had never refused a hurdle in my life. Armed with a torch (very tiny, given to me by Chanel when I had to look at their new jewellery collection in a darkened grotto in Paris), I gingerly unlocked the Wendy House door. There, blinking in the sudden light, was Susie!

'It's her! It's Susie!!' I yelled. 'Fetch water and the cat basket!!' I swear a cheer went up from all the neighbours watching the commotion from their bedroom windows. I had to empty the Wendy House of its contents – prams, tiny chairs, hideous dolls – before I could squeeze myself in with the basket. I held out the bowl of water to my Susie and she had a good lap. How I caught her I don't know – it was like one of those cartoons where the cat is a blur, with various claws emerging from the whirlwind – but at last I managed to stuff her in the basket and hand her carefully over the fence to The Husband, who was hopping and crying and laughing.

When I finally got back and went upstairs to where he was trying to feed her under the bed, I noticed she was covered in blood. 'Don't worry,' he said, 'that's all your blood.' I hadn't noticed in the commotion that she had shredded my arms.

She is now confined to barracks, dining on poached cod and salmon and organic chicken and bottled flat water, while she puts on weight. She hasn't yet said where she has been. She does look very thin, the Kate Moss of the cat world, but other than that none the worse for wear, if a bit smelly. The Husband says she was on the cat equivalent of a gap year. Last night, she stood on my chest, kneading my lovely Hanro vest shouting for her biscuits as usual, while Squeaky was wedged, paws in the air and snoring loudly, between us. 'My life is no longer my own,' The Husband said. 'I spent all day changing cat litter, trying to persuade Susie to eat her sustainably fished salmon. I'm absolutely exhausted. I haven't even had time for a shower today.'

Oh dear.

Chapter 58

AUGUST 15, 2004

WHAT COULD BE MORE PERFECT:

A FILM ABOUT WHALES AND RIDING?

'How about a film this weekend?' I said. 'I'd really like to see *The Story of the Weeping Camel.*'

'No, I don't fancy that,' he said. He never wants to see the films I want to, like *Whale Rider*. He only wants to see obscure documentaries about Fog and War.

I mooted we could go to an exhibition. 'I am never going to a gallery with you again,' he said. 'At Tate Modern, you kept saying you had gone blind with hunger, and had to sit down, and we'd only been there ten minutes.'

'That is because I was wearing the wrong shoes,' I said crossly.

I told him I at least wanted him to be nice to me this weekend. 'When am I not nice?' he demanded indignantly.

'Well, last weekend you said my vegetable lasagne was raw, and you kept interrupting while I was watching *Kind Hearts and Coronets.*'

Men are so transparent, aren't they? On Tuesday, he phoned me at work to say sorry that he hadn't made cheese on toast for me when I got home at eleven the night before; he was already in bed, fast asleep. 'Oh, that's okay,' I said.

But then he continued with, 'Would you mind if I went to Ibiza for two weeks with David?'

'What, with me as well?'

'Well, you can never take the time off, can you? And it will be my last opportunity to go clubbing and get drunk before we get a baby.'

Which brings me to two important topics about The Husband that are concerning my mum, sister, Kerry and Robi. 'Gorgeous though he is,' said Robi, 'he does seem rather expensive and useless.'

'I'd say no to him going to Ibiza. How is he going to pay for it? Tell him to get a job,' said Kerry.

I admit. He does have a rather relaxed attitude towards life. On Monday, I asked him to pick up my dry-cleaning. At 7 p.m. he phoned to say that they shut at 7.30 p.m., so he could get there if he rushed, but he had to feed the cats, and could he go tomorrow instead? I have resigned myself to the fact I will never see my cream Prada again.

'I'm so useless, Lizzie,' he said. 'You could do so much better than me.'

But he has some good qualities: he makes me laugh, and is very good with his step-pets and one whole pet. This is the email he sent me on Tuesday morning:

'Have managed to coax Susie indoors, and she is sat on the bed eating her breakfast… a cod and biscuit platter. She is v grown up now and comes when I call her. Am in attendance should she require cuddles. xx'

He sends lovely texts out of the blue, viz: 'I luv u Chubby. xx'

Worrying topic number two for my friends and family is my aptitude for being a parent. They keep trying to impress upon me how much hard work a baby is going to be.

'You will no longer be able to go out, or have intelligent conversations, or mini breaks,' said Kerry.

'What about the mess?' said my friend whose little boy's latest hobby is to do potato prints on the walls. Isn't it odd none of them talk about the joy, the love, only the stickiness?

Chapter 59

AUGUST 28, 2004

HE INEXPLICABLY BUYS A BUTTER DISH

The question The Husband asks most often is: 'Who do you love more, Lizzie? Me or Squeaky?' I tell him I love them exactly the same. 'But how can you love Squeaky as much as me; she is just a cat, and she never does anything.'

'She does loads. She head butts. She can use the phone.'

But, to be honest, I love the cats a weeny bit more than him. Cats have many advantages over mere men...

1. When we first got Susie, even though she had never lived in a house, she knew how to use the litter tray. She smells sweet. The Husband, on the other hand, often doesn't flush the loo; he would, were it not for my intervention, still be using the same toothbrush he had when Spurs were near the top of the league.

2. Cats enjoy a lie-in with their mummy at weekends. It is one of the great pleasures in life, along with Vanilla (not coffee) Walnut Whips, Bounty Ice Cream and Arctic Roll. At weekends (a real departure from his behaviour during the week), The Husband gets up very noisily at dawn and spends several hours crashing around downstairs. It is like having a flatmate who doesn't pay rent.

3. In the middle of the night, if there is a loud bang, the cats are up, alert, tails in the air like chimney sweeps, anxious expressions on their faces. He is fast asleep, snoring gently, occasionally grinding his teeth.

4. Cats never, ever criticise. Only love shines in their big, dark eyes. The Husband recently said he hates me in tracky bottoms; there was that comment about my hair being like a helmet; the wild

stab at 11 stone; he criticises my choice of reading matter (Maggie O'Farrell's *After You'd Gone*. 'What's that about? [in a high-pitched voice] He said this and she said that...').

Anyway, I don't think he really loves me. For a start, he keeps shutting himself behind closed doors. When he was sitting at his computer the other day, and I went to sit next to him (please bear in mind I work a 60-hour week; I could be a brain surgeon if I had more skills), he said, 'Can't you just give me half an hour on my own?'

He makes me watch cricket and then gets all cross when I say, 'Isn't it sweet they wear jumpers.' When he is serving dinner, he always gives me less than he has, and thinks I don't notice. He never gives me a back massage. And in bed, just when I have got to a particularly exciting bit in *The Time Traveler's Wife*, he makes me switch the light off. He refuses point blank to go in the loft. He is driving me crazy. So, listen, Aston Kutcher. I am going on strike. As Super Nanny says, it isn't good to reward bad behaviour with cuddles.

And do you know what, for one brief second, it worked! I got an email at work.

'Chubby! Have been shopping and bought:

Large chrome French press for two

New Dualit all-chrome toaster (v expensive!)

Butter dish

Two breakfast mugs

Wine plug

Olive oil bottle stop thingy

Food, including water that is not too fizzy

Also, met old man who lives across the road (the one with the green Fiat); he said his cat died last week... she was 27 years old. He was v sad and started crying.'

Goodness. What a turn up. This is someone who has never purchased so much as a dishcloth. Who had only ever drunk coffee in granules. When I got home, he said he had started to feel all domesticated and to actually enjoy having nice things around him, not festering ones.

Then, on Tuesday, he went out with his friend Caroline and when I got home, instead of finding chopping boards in the sink and his gym kit steaming, I found he had made me a free-range egg bap and left it in the fridge. I began to wonder if he had thrown his *FHM High Street Honeys* in the wheelie bin. When he got home, he greeted me like a labrador after a long, wet walk.

'Why are you being so nice to me?' I asked.

'Can't I be nice to my lovely wife?'

'But you are usually so horrid.'

'I'm not horrid. You are never going to find another man who knows that Squeaky likes coley but hates cod, who recycles, who is always on vulnerable sleeping puss alert, who told the postman not to smudge our letter box, and who never puts your undies in the washing machine.'

I cannot believe he had been listening all along.

Chapter 60

SEPTEMBER 12, 2004
I SUFFER FROM HURRIED WOMAN SYNDROME

Okay. So last week we had the joy of the all-chrome Dualit toaster and the olive oil bottle stop thingy. Well, come Friday, we'd had an awful row. We'd planned to go to the Cotswolds for a mini break that Saturday morning, and on Friday I phoned The Husband to tell him that I had invited my friends, Sue and Henry, and their little boy along too.

He went all silent. 'Why didn't you ask me first?' he asked.

'I didn't think you'd mind.'

'But I wanted to have a weekend with just the two of us, lazing around naked on the lawn, chatting under the stars...'

Oh. I don't do naked. I have just had a week off, and he spent most of the time working on his book, something he hasn't done for the past few months, but which he miraculously took up when I was home all day. We didn't do anything remotely romantic: I went in to town to choose a cooker, had the windows cleaned, and went to the dentist. We went out to dinner once, but only stayed out for a grand total of one hour as he wanted to get home to see the Copa America final.

But – and here is the BIG but, something I am sure Dr Laura Schlessinger, author of *The Proper Care and Feeding of Husbands* would not approve of – rather than apologising for asking another couple along with their child (who although sweet on the brief occasions we have met it before turned out to be THE CHILD FROM HELL) I went on the offensive.

'Well,' I said. 'When I had a week's holiday, you disappeared with no prior notice with your friend for the day and stayed for dinner, and then on the Friday morning, you stuck your head out the back door – I was having coffee, alone, in the garden; why is it you don't like the garden, by the way, and only ever sit in it while you're having a fag? – and said you were going to see your mum, and I didn't hear from you again until 9.20 p.m. when you called to say you were on your way home and that you had already eaten, so I had to have pasta with NOTHING on top.'

I think The Husband takes me for granted. The most common thing I say to him is, 'I bet you don't speak to David/Bunmi/Rick/Caroline the way you speak to me.'

This is usually after he has whined up the stairs, 'Lizzie!! What have you done with the spatula/my white T-shirt/the mayonnaise?'

Anyway, next weekend he is off to Ibiza for a week to chill by the sea, go clubbing, read books, and practise three hours of yoga every morning. Let's see how much he misses me. Let's see how he gets on with nobody to hire the car, navigate, drive, find his sunglasses and remember the sun cream. I think the reason I invited another couple along for the weekend was that I assumed he wouldn't want to spend time on his own with me (viz, my disastrous week off). I feel like Mrs Drudge. I have Hurried Woman Syndrome (thank you, Dr Schlessinger) in that I spend so much time paying bills/washing/taking Snoopy to the vet I never have time to do the things I used to do, like spend an evening watching *Frasier*. Do you know, he even asked me to buy him some sunglasses (he'd lost the pair I gave him) and pick up some toothpaste and dental floss for his holiday the next time I'm in Boots. It's time he stopped treating me like his mum. And for my part, I am not going to take him to the airport or pack his trunks. I promise.

SEPTEMBER 19, 2004
I TELL HIM HE NEEDS TO FIND SOMEONE YOUNGER

One minute you are trolling along, popping to the Conran Shop to buy an all-chrome juicer. Actually, I was going to tell you about my raw food/fresh juice week-long detox, combined with body brushing and liver-cleansing vitamins that are as big as horse pills. And then, bam! Change of plan.

It all started last Sunday, when The Husband and I went to meet my friend Meena's parents, who are going to help us in India with the adoption plans. We chatted for a while, and made tentative plans to travel to the Punjab at the end of October for a recce. Then we went to the pub with my friend for a drink. I noticed The Husband was staring at his beer through his incredibly long eyelashes, but didn't think much of it. On the Monday I received an email from Meena saying, 'Was Nirpal OK? He seemed to go a bit quiet afterwards...xxxxxxx'

Then, on Thursday evening, while we were watching a documentary on TV about an undercover childcare worker in a nursery, he suddenly said, 'I'm not sure I'm ready to do this.' I turned the sound off. 'One minute I said that I might one day want to be a dad, and the next we were going through the adoption process, and making plans to go to India.' What does he mean, one day? When we had made the initial decision he had said he was going to get a job the next day! If I had left it to him to contact Social Services it would never have happened, like the lawn never being mowed.

'Well, I thought you wanted to get things moving...it could still take a year,' I said pathetically.

'But I could afford to wait five or six years,' he said. 'I'm still only thirty [does he age at some weird slow rate, whereas I age in dog years?]. To be honest, I'm feeling a bit scared about becoming a dad…I've got a lot going on in my head at the moment. My best friend is really sick, and she is someone I turn to for guidance more than anyone else. You have had many more years than I've had to get ready for this. I just don't know what I want. I know you'd be a really good mum, and that you need to do it now, but I don't want to ruin a little baby's life…'

'You shouldn't do something because I want you to,' I said calmly. 'To be honest, I've been looking forward to it, to doing something with more meaning, rather than just going out to work for a change.'

We talked for a bit, and I pointed out that he had had four years of complete freedom to do his own thing. And then he said, giving me a cuddle, 'No. Do you know what, let's do it. I want to do it. The little girl can have the room next to ours, and I'll go swimming really early so I'm back for 7.30 when she wakes up…'

But I've decided. I'm not going to clutch at straws like I usually do and try really, really hard and hope things turn out for the best. I told him something I'd been thinking for ages.

'I think you should find someone younger,' I said.

He said nothing.

My feeling is, if you love someone, things might not be perfect but you compromise. Maybe he will be ready in six years' time to have a child, but maybe he won't be with the love of his life then, or maybe she'll turn out to be a pain in the bum, or demand he buys a BMW and then she'll have an affair with Sven Goran Eriksson, I don't know. I'm thinking of becoming a Buddhist, so that my happiness will come from within, and not be subject to outside forces. Anyway, tomorrow The Husband is off to Ibiza for a week. We'll see what happens when he gets back.

Chapter 61

SEPTEMBER 26, 2004

WENT 2 IBIZA TOWN 4 DIN. BOUGHT U A PRES XX

I drove him to the airport so that he could catch his flight to Ibiza (I know, I know), and in the car he squeezed my knee and said, 'I don't think you realise how much I love you.'

When I dropped him off, I felt all teary. On the way home, I bought two DVDs to watch while he's away: *The Complete Second Series of Frasier*, and *Mystic River*. I couldn't understand a word anyone said in *Mystic River*, had no idea who had been murdered or why, and gave up before the end. He could have explained everything. Over the next few days, I received the following text messages:

'Am in Ibiza! missing u. wot is pin 4 credit card?'

'luv u chubby. Must come here together 1 day. hug the cats 4 me. xx'

'Feel like I've had a hol now. am missing u. x'

'Went 2 Ibiza town 4 din. was lovely. bought u a pres. xx'

Then, on Thursday night, he called me and we had a long chat. He was sitting on the beach and I could hear the waves breaking in the background.

'I really love you, you know,' he said. I told him I loved him too, and offered to put Squeaky on. I held the phone to her little mouth but she remained silent.

'I don't know why she's not talking,' I said. 'Maybe she is cross with you for not being around.'

'No, she only talks to you because I give her a poke,' he said.

'You don't poke her! You mustn't poke the cats!'

'Course I don't. She talks to you because she hears your voice and she loves you.'

I think it has been good for us to have a week apart. (The only weird thing was getting home and finding the packaging for a pair of eyelash curlers; why would he need to curl his eyelashes on a yoga holiday?) I had been thinking that maybe I would enjoy being on my own again, but after a week of M&S pasta sauce, watching *About Last Night* in bed on Sunday morning (what was Demi Moore thinking with those clothes and that hairstyle? She wore a shirt decorated with a pack of cards!), trying to feed Susie before leaving for work at 7.30 a.m. ('Susie, come down from the tree, it's your favourite! Please, darling'), sleeping diagonally in the bed (Squeaky has enjoyed a whole section to herself) while wearing Bliss Softening Socks with Softening Sock Salve, I have got bored of being single. Nothing is fun without him. I couldn't enjoy juicing a pineapple for the first time in my whizzy new machine (I bought it from the Conran Shop with potential new baby in mind; then Jackie at work told me babies don't drink fruit juice as it rots their teeth), or even seeing Madonna live at Earls Court (The Husband would have had a first-hand demonstration of how bendy a woman over forty can actually be).

He is flying back tomorrow. In preparation, I have sprayed myself all over with something called Airbrush in a Can, bought happy eggs, organic milk and a lovely wholemeal loaf from a tiny patisserie (none of your supermarket rubbish) and lit aromatherapy candles. I wonder what my present is.

Anyway, tonight I am going to sleep propped up on pillows to avoid puffy eyes. Squeaky has been combed. Snoopy has a new collar. I am so excited, it's as if I'm about to go on a first date. I hope he still fancies me!

Chapter 62

OCTOBER 3, 2004
I PUT HIS BASEBALL CAP IN THE WASHING MACHINE

After he got back from Ibiza, all tanned and bendy after a week of yoga on the beach ('I was the only man there with Dr Hauschka suntan lotion'), we decided to go to the Big Apple for a few days. During the flight, I was telling him a story about my first trip to New York (during which I had been too scared to leave my room) when I realised that the reason he was smiling was because he was wearing earplugs. He removed one. 'I must bring these home with me,' he said, grinning.

We stayed at the Mandarin Oriental, which was fabulous. Our room was on the 52nd floor, with a view of Central Park. It was perfect, except...

On our first night, I had booked dinner at Soho House in the Meatpacking District. I thought he would like the restaurant because it was owned by the same people as Babington House. Before dinner, we went upstairs for a drink at the roof bar by the pool (where *Sex and the City* was filmed). Then we went down to the restaurant. It was full of beautiful people in expensive clothes. He moaned that the 'only person of colour' in there, apart from him, was the waiter.

'That is not true,' I said. 'Ozwald Boateng is over there. He's black.'

'Fashion designers don't count.'

A swift hour and fifteen minutes later, we stumbled out into the New York night to hail a cab. 'That place was horrible,' he said. 'Just like all those places we go to in London.' I rummaged in my bag for a $20 bill for the fare and handed it to him. 'Why don't you deal with it?' he said, turning to look out the window.

The next morning, I woke to see the sun rise behind Trump Tower (which is brown and very seventies). The Husband was nowhere to be found, so I ordered breakfast on my own. Turns out he went for a swim in the hotel spa and then a wander.

That afternoon, we took a cab downtown because I wanted to browse in the new Prada store. I saw a beautiful bag, a pair of pin-stripe trousers and a shirt with bracelet sleeves. He looked at the price tag and nearly turned white with shock. 'Why on earth do you want to spend all that money?'

We walked up town, and in the process he bought five pairs of jeans and six books. 'I won't fit these soon,' he said, swinging his bags, 'not if I keep up the Astanga yoga classes.'

We met my friend Emma (she of the Marmite), for dinner at an Italian restaurant on East 47th street. She had lost loads of weight, and was obviously in love (with an actor; she flies down to LA every other weekend). She showed me pictures of Perry, her 9/11 cat (his owner never came home). As we walked back to our hotel (after stopping in Starbucks so that he could spend a penny), The Husband said, 'Didn't Emma look beautiful?'

The following day, he said he wanted to go to Harlem, so we took a taxi there, had a really greasy breakfast in a famous soul food restaurant and then walked back to our hotel through Central Park. It was boiling. I saw a *Vogue* fashion shoot taking place with an absolutely stunning chestnut horse. We had ice cream. It was okay, but he never once held my hand, or told me I looked nice. We went back to the hotel, had a swim to freshen up, and then got a taxi to the airport. I kept smiling at him in New York (which was hard after he had sent a messenger out to buy him a pair of swimming goggles;

I, apparently, had forgotten to pack his). He didn't ever smile back.

Back in London, I fed the pussies (whom I had missed dreadfully; H had looked after them, as she is the only person, after me and The Husband, Susie will deign to go near), unpacked the suitcase (the part I really hate about going away) and did four million loads of washing.

'Why?' said The Husband later, 'did you put my brand new baseball cap in the washing machine? Now it is all bent out of shape.'

'I will get you a new one,' I said, folding a towel carefully, hating the person he has made me become.

Chapter 63

OCTOBER 9, 2004
WE ARE APPROVED AS POTENTIAL PARENTS, BUT HE DOESN'T KNOW OR CARE

Today is the day our case goes before the adoption panel. I doubt he has even remembered. Marie phones me, excited, at 4 p.m. 'You made it!' she shouts excitedly above the traffic on Mare Street. 'You've been approved! Now you can start to get that baby. You will give someone such a beautiful life.'

I thank her for everything she has done for us. I sit at my desk and cry. I don't even bother phoning to tell him.

Chapter 64

SQUEAKY HAS FORGOTTEN HOW TO BE A CAT

Another glorious weekend in the Jones household. Saturday: today we start counselling. No, not me and The Husband; me and my cats. I have just read a brilliant book called *Cat Confidential, the Book your Cat Would Want you to Read*, by Vicky Halls, in which she outlines how we can make our cats' lives happier and more fulfilled. I booked a consultation, telling her I thought we had two problem areas: namely, Susie, who has 'sudden onset fear', and Squeaky, who is, as far as I could ascertain from the book, seriously 'over-bonded' (and seriously overweight, and a bit narky).

I am sitting in the garden with Vicky, and the only cat who bothers to show up is Squeaky, who loves to join in, especially if we are talking about her. Vicky asks me to describe our relationship. 'Well, Squeak is basically a person. She watches TV – her favourite programme is *Animal Hospital*, she loves Rolf Harris – and she sits in the bathroom while I have a bath, she is on the draining board when I wash up, and the moment she hears my electric toothbrush at night she goes up and gets in to bed. She is very talkative...'

At this point, The Husband, who had thought I was bonkers for consulting a cat psychiatrist, joins us to say: 'Which is really annoying, because she sleeps exactly in my spot and won't budge, which means I have to sleep in a weird croissant shape around her, and it's also really hot...'

'Liz, would you say Squeaky is annoying in bed?' asks Vicky.

'She does tend to knead the linen duvet cover, and in the morning she stands on my head and dribbles and it's really painful, and she won't stop licking me with her little rasping tongue, but it's not a huge problem…'

Her weight, though, clearly is. She has started to find it hard to climb stairs, and negotiate the cat flap. 'The reason she is overweight,' says Vicky authoritatively, 'is that she has forgotten how to be a cat. She is too reliant on you, and has nothing to do all day apart from sleep [at this point, I look over at The Husband, who looks as though he is about to start whistling and playing in the soil with his foot] and wait for you to get home. She needs to be on a strict diet, and to start taking exercise, which means you have to play with her for twenty minutes, twice a day.'

'You see,' says The Husband, all happy. 'This is what I have been telling you all along. You are always saying [the high-pitched voice again], "Oh, she's so happy, she loves her mummy." But she isn't happy, it's not natural for her to be so bonded; you have to be cruel to be kind. You are too soft. You worry too much, about the tabbies when they are off doing their own thing, about Squeaky feeling left out when the others are having chicken…'

Vicky, by now looking quite alarmed, leaves, having not laid eyes on Snoop or Sue. Her advice about picking up Susie to take her to the vet, possibly in an emergency, is that I leave the task to The Husband, who says I transmit my anxiety, and to be strict with Squeaky, who is now looking very glum indeed. I haven't even told Vicky about Squeaky's nipple rash (they rub on the floor). But I will miss having someone to watch *Pet Rescue* with, and who grunts with pleasure when I put my key in the door.

Chapter 65

MY PETS, IN CHRONOLOGICAL ORDER

1. Pompey. Golden retriever, rescued when he was two. Definitely 'over-bonded' with my dad. Was always escaping to cross the very dangerous A road to have sex with the bitches on the housing estate; I once saw his willy – pink, like one of my mum's lipsticks – as a child and was deeply shocked. When the vet had to put him down for being too old, my dad cried, and I cried too, deeply ashamed I was more upset than when Granny Jones died.

2. Penny. White rabbit with pink eyes. Rescued from a rabbit farm. Very vicious, probably because she was kept in a cage (how was I to know? I was a child). Liked toast. I lived in mortal fear she would catch myxomatosis.

3. Guinea. A guinea pig with a tan bottom, bought from my friend Penny Cresswell. Ah. Penny Cresswell. One Sunday, Penny (the eight-year-old girl, not the white rabbit) and her parents knocked at my front door and asked if I wanted to go to the zoo. I said okay, and shut the door. I went and had Sunday lunch, and pudding and custard. There was another, louder knock. Them again. Ah. I hadn't realised they meant right now. I often berate my mum for not giving me any social graces whatsoever. Guinea died one Friday evening during an episode of *The Virginian*.

4. Labby. The black labrador. Bought when I answered an ad in *The Times* placed by a Russian lesbian. I gave her to my dad, who loved her almost as much as he loved my mum. She loved sitting on the sofa watching TV. Eventually got cancer and my dad cried again. He said he hadn't even cried when everyone apart from him was killed when their Churchill tank was blown up in Italy.

5. Monty. My horse. Bay, 16.2 hands. Vicious. Once bit me on the arm (I still have the scar) when I was only trying to heighten his hay net. Used to walk me in to nettle patches. Was prone to refusing jumps. Died of old age after happy retirement with a pony. What is it about girls and ponies? I have a pile of paperbacks upstairs: *Jill's Gymkhana, Jill had two ponies, A stable for Jill, Jill's Pony Trek, I had two ponies, We Hunted Hounds, Goodbye to Hounds, Riders from Afar....* Every year I would enter the WH Smith short-story competition to win a pony. I was always very badly let down.

6. The pussies. You have met them already.

Chapter 66

I haven't told you what happened on my birthday... first of all

SEPTEMBER 4, 2004
MY BIRTHDAY EVE

I had arranged to meet Kerry for lunch ('My treat!' she kept piping) at the Organic Pub, but felt sorry for The Husband so invited him along too. I had secretly arranged to view a house round the corner from there, and as we parked I told him this. He merely said, 'Okay, I'll see you in the pub.'

The estate agent showed me round, and although the place was a tip, I knew it could be gorgeous. I started to imagine what I could do with the place. After all, I had bought my house in'96 and felt ready for a change. I wanted to live in a nicer area and have a bit more space, especially with a baby.... I took the details with me, and walked round to the restaurant. Kerry arrived (she tried not to register surprise that The Husband was with me) and we got a table outside.

'I think we want a bottle of Albet y Noya,' The Husband said. 'And I will have the monkfish, but can I have it with green beans and mash, not fennel.' (Does he not know it is rude not to let us order first?) Anyway, Kerry and I chattered away about how annoying work is and he kept interrupting, and swearing a lot. I showed her the house details.

'Kevin and I are thinking of buying a wreck,' she said, excited for me. 'Maybe we could live round here too.'

'Well,' The Husband said. 'I think you are bonkers. You want to take on renovating a house that doesn't even have heating, as well as adopt a child, and maybe leave your job and go freelance. You are not in touch with f***ing reality.'

Kerry looked shocked. She had never seen him like this before. She changed the subject. I wouldn't let her pay the bill. He gave the waiter his debit card, but it was brought back, hopelessly out of date.

SEPTEMBER 5, 2004
MY BIRTHDAY, WHEN IF I WANT TO KNOW WHAT HARD WORK IS I SHOULD TALK TO HIS MUM

Sunday. Today is my birthday. It is a date that doesn't always turn out to be the happiest square on the calendar. To be honest – which, as we will learn later, is not, apparently, one of my best qualities – it is the extra pressure this day puts on The Husband, to provide a card and a small gift and to be reasonably nice, that forces him to go on the offensive. I know something is brewing, but it isn't my morning Illy coffee with Evian.

After waking up I go downstairs to find he has gone swimming, so I make myself some Neal's Yard muesli and sit in the garden, reading. Later, as I am running my bath, he arrives home, laden with shopping. 'I am going to make you salad for lunch, then take you out to dinner, and this,' he says, disappearing out to the car, and returning with a lily in a pot, 'is for you.' (I later find out he bought the shopping and the lily in a pot on my credit card.)

I love my b-day. I sit outside reading the papers while he is indoors on his computer, then at about 5 p.m. I start getting ready to go out. I am wondering what to wear when he appears and says, 'How about a Mediterranean supper in the garden?' (I never got the salad for lunch.) I say that is fine, perfect, as long as we eat outside and not in front of the TV, although I am slightly disappointed. Over pitta bread and hummus, we chat about the cats and their therapy, and then he tells me that the thing that annoys him most about me is that I am so dishonest.

'How can you even think about buying another house?' he asks. Then he says that he isn't ready to be a father, that the 'world is just opening up for me; soon I am going to be a published author'. That although I have supported him all these years, he has also been a support to me (When? How?) and that if I want to know what hard work is, I should talk to his mum.

Then he says (and please try to remember this is on my birthday; no wonder I have a complex about age), 'Are you trying to adopt a child because you are frightened of losing me?' It is his passing shot. (Later, I think about this question honestly. And no, I am not frightened of losing him. Losing what? Someone who consistently undermines me, saps my strength, makes cheap jokes about my age?) He says he will go ahead and have a child with me 'as a compromise'.

I tell him did he really think Michelle said to Jamie, 'Come on Jamie, give up your ambitions as a rock megastar, I want us to have twins.' I tell him most men don't get a bloody option; it just happens and they have to deal with it, or they don't and they leave.

I don't want us changing some little girl's life, giving her a future, to be a compromise. I am not frightened of losing him. To be honest, for the past few months he has been doing his own thing, getting on with his life, doing yoga practice every morning in Bethnal Green, working on his novel, and I have been going to work every day. I don't have a life any more. As long as I don't demand anything, such as, 'Please glue the bathroom tap,' everything is just fine and dandy thank you.

I have encouraged him to travel. I never ask him to pay for anything. I can spend the whole week at home doing nothing and it still costs me money, for nightclubs I never go to, beer I never drink, books I never read, places I never see, jeans I never wear that will soon be discarded for a pair in a smaller size. But what if I asked him to finance me while I spent six months (not five years) writing a book? Do you know what his reply to this question was, on my birthday? Only if he thought my book was 'good enough'.

But I know, I know. He does have a point. I want to renovate houses and get a baby, and he is only thirty. I am standing in his way. I sent an email to Kerry on the Monday, apologising for his behaviour yesterday, saying I am not sure he even likes me any more. 'I know!' she wrote back. 'I have never seen him like that. He was miserable and kept swearing. I felt so sorry for you.'

That night, unable to sleep, I write him an email in my head:
'I think we should put off adopting for now. You should get your

book published, earn some money, go to New Zealand. Why don't you just leave mowing the lawn for now…. I will phone Jeremy the gardener. Why don't you decide whether or not you want to be with me at all.'

Chapter 67

SEPTEMBER 24, 2004
IS IT NORMAL NOT TO KNOW, AT ALL,
WHAT IS GOING ON IN THE OTHER PERSON'S HEAD?

I have been pondering over the past few weeks what to do next. His words (on my birthday!), 'I have changed since I met you. I've got no idea what I want to be doing over the next few years', have been ringing in my ears. To be honest, I think it's pathetic. Who is more attractive: Brad Pitt married to the lovely Jennifer Aniston, or Brad Pitt, post their separation? What on earth could The Husband mean? He wants to go travelling? This is the person who asked me to consult my A to Z when he was on his way to Soho in a BLACK TAXI! But, stupid old me, still wounded from the David Scrace non affair, didn't have the courage to squeak those fatal words, 'Do you mean you want us to split up?'

So I am terribly sorry, but I still don't know what is happening between us. Let's make a summary of my gripes and niggles and 3 a.m. worries.

1. He now says he is too young to adopt a child. He might be, but I am not.

2. He does seem to prefer spending time with his friends to going

to dinner with me. On Saturday, he went to a party and didn't invite me along, so I stayed home and watched the American Civil War drama *North and South* on video (the one in which Patrick Swayze has a limp and keeps meeting Lesley Anne Down for difficult romantic trysts).

3. I can't make plans for the future: whether to move house, downscale my workload, book flights to India to visit the orphanage, buy half a pint of organic Rachel's skimmed milk or a pint. Nothing. My thinking was, you get married and then you go on a journey, seeing what pops up and sorting it out together. I feel quite alone, to be honest, which is odd when you are sleeping right next to someone and picking up his socks and rubbing his grubby fingerprints off the remote control.

4. The bonuses of having a husband seem to be quite absent at the mo. I have had to ring a marvellous firm called Handyman.co.uk to ask them to come and fix all the niggly, annoying things around the house. I always thought having a husband would mean: a) a firm hot date on your birthday and Valentine's Day; and b) someone to talk over your problems with, who is on your side, no matter what. Sadly, this hasn't turned out to be the case.

As well as pondering all of the above, I have been thinking really stupid things, such as, if we split up, how will I break it to Farmaround.co.uk that my weekly delivery of luxury organic fruit and veg should be discontinued? (I have no idea what to do with kale, for example, or things that come in furry pods.)

And what about the cats? Would he only take Susie out on a Sunday and leave the other two languishing at home in front of the television?

But maybe I am getting things out of proportion. I read my horoscope the other day, and it said: 'If you are having relationship problems, relax. Only a perfectionist like you would expect every-thing to be sweetness and light all the time. All couples argue. It's normal.'

But is it normal not to know, at all, what is going on in the other person's head? Sometimes he is so wrapped up in himself it seems as if he doesn't know I am there, or care if I am alive. Snoopy has much better manners. When he walks into a room he does a little chirrup that says, 'Here I am!' and so I say hello and tickle his head and pull his tail. Small gestures, the chirrup and the tickle, but what we are both saying is, 'Hello, darling. I want to be near you and I love you.'

If The Husband disappears to the spare bedroom with the phone and slams the door one more time I think I will be tempted to pick up the extension and chirrup, 'I live here too! My feelings matter! Why am I being ignored?!'

I have consulted, of course, Kerry and Jeremy. Kerry emailed me:

'Oh Lizzie. I know it's hard to play games, but I think you should be distant for a while. Don't do anything for him. See how he likes that.'

And Jerry? He simply said: 'Easy come, easy go.'

Chapter 68

THE FIRST TWO WEEKS IN OCTOBER 2004
I CAN NO LONGER PLOUGH MY WAY
THROUGH FRASIER BOX SETS

I really, really don't want to be single again. But it can happen to the best of us. Look at Cameron Diaz and Justin Timberlake. One minute they are nibbling each other's ears at basketball matches, the next they are 'on a break'. The newspapers keep citing the fact that she is 11 years older than he is. Are they mad? She is Cameron Diaz! He is a curly haired nerd. She is much more of a catch than he is. And over the past week I have been thinking that, even if I can remember the days when tank tops and plum eyeshadow were the height of fashion, I am a bit of a catch too, actually, and deserve to be treated as such.

I have been weighing up the pros and cons of being married as opposed to being single.

Being married means:

1. You wear a wedding ring. This is very reassuring when you are out and about of a Sunday morning sans make-up, with toothpaste stains on your T-shirt from the night before, and you are shuffling because you borrowed your husband's giant flip-flops. When the young man in the newsagent gives you a look that says, 'Have you escaped from somewhere?' you flash him the ring as you pay for the papers. See, I am not a mad woman; somebody loves me.

2. When you speak to men on the phone about installing the new stainless-steel range/mending the tumble dryer/mowing the lawn and they say, Is that Miss or Mrs?, you are able to say, Mrs, thank

you very much. It's just that my husband is far too busy to do manual work...

3. Ummm...

Being single means:

1. You can spend all of Sunday in your PJs, eating things out of packets, ploughing your way through *Frasier* box sets and *Seabiscuit*. Never, ever will someone seize the remote control to turn the channel to watch La Liga / Serie A / the History Channel...

2. You live in hope. You can always comfort yourself with the distinct possibility that George Clooney will get bored of old Lisa Snowdon and give you a call.

3. You see more of your girlfriends. Last Saturday, I went to see the new Tom Cruise movie with my friend Robina and we giggled so much my Diet Coke came out of my nose. That never happens with a husband.

Anyway, tomorrow we are flying to Mauritius for a week. As my mum said, 'Let's see if he behaves on holiday.' In preparation, I have packed two novels – the new ones by Louis de Bernieres and Kate Atkinson; The Husband says only that he is bringing 'some philosophy' – some Dr Hauschka factor 50 (sunbathing is terribly ageing; perhaps The Husband should go without and catch up), and a new black bikini. I have had my hair coloured, my legs waxed and my eyelashes tinted. I have given four A4 sheets of instructions to the cat sitter. One last thing. It's really weird, but when The Husband went to Ibiza without me he ironed T-shirts and washed trainers and bought exfoliating body scrubs like there was no tomorrow. Going away with me he has thrown a toothbrush in to my case and said he 'might pick up a T-shirt at the airport'. I asked him why, and he said, 'Well, I don't have to impress you any more, do I?'

Well, dear reader, all I can say is that HE SO DOES...

Postcard I sent to Kerry from Mauritius
'Hi Kez, how is work? It keeps raining, and there are more Premiership games on here than at home. Hope your sister is okay after being robbed at gunpoint in her house... will she come home from LA now do you think? Hubby being very elusive, which is quite hard on a desert island. Not really talking to me, what's new? We haven't had sex but I have had a Lomi Lomi massage – she used her elbows! Love to you and Kev,

L xxxxx'

Chapter 69

OCTOBER 8, 2004
WE HAVE A BLAZING ROW OVER THE LATTES

We were in a coffee shop in Upper Street on Saturday having an argument. I think what started it was that I had taken him to see a lovely terraced house nearby, and although he told the lady owner that he thought it was 'beautiful', the moment we walked out the front door he said it had 'a really bad vibe'. He said he doesn't want to move, that he never had anywhere he felt was home before because his parents kept moving and not decorating, and that he doesn't want to do anything that causes him 'a headache'.

Anyway, slurping his full-fat latte, he said, 'Why do you think I put on three stone last summer?' I'm thinking: choccie biccies; Pringles; custard creams; Hill Station ice cream; sandwiches; my leftovers. I didn't say a word, but merely waited for him to tell me.

'Because you made me depressed, with your constant wailing about being tired. You might think I'm the baby in this relationship but I'm not, you're the baby. I've supported you more – emotionally – than you have supported me.' (I dispute that. When I have complained about my job, his response has been a disinterested, 'Well, quit then', which I can't because who would pay the mortgage?) Then he continued, 'You might think you pay for everything but listen, I'm cheap at the price.'

'You're not cheap,' I replied, thinking of all the times he gets taxis because it's cold or because it would mean driving his PERFECT-LY GOOD CAR on the dual carriageway, or when he orders a glass of wine and doesn't finish it, or buys loads of magazines at the airport and doesn't read them. 'I could have a horse instead of you.'

'I don't have to go to yoga three times a week,' he said (it is £9 a session). 'We don't have to eat out all the time.'

'But I like going out,' I said. 'I don't want to just go to work and come home and sit in a cold hovel eating things from the big freezer place. Why should I?' (I almost said, 'I'm tired!')

'You are always saying, "I'm worth it [he puts on a really horrid baby voice], I deserve to be spoilt." Why can you never have a bath with just water?'

'So, what you are saying is, I have to pay for my relationship, which I am jolly lucky to have,' I said.

The argument ended with him saying, 'I don't know that we are good for each other.'

That night, I dropped the huge chopping board on my big toe. I started wailing hot tears and after about nine hours he sloped down to 'see what all the noise was about'. I told him that he could at least be sympathetic. He merely replied, 'If I went crying to my mum over my big toe, she would have given me a clip round the ear and said, "Here, now you've got something to cry about."'

That's not very nice. I suddenly want my mum. I am going to have a black nail, and then it is going to fall off and it will ruin the effect of my feet. I went to bed, emotionally exhausted, like a toddler who has spent all day screaming on the floor. He ruined my weekend – again!

THE NEXT DAY AT WORK

I draft an email.

'Hi darling. I am sure you are right about not taking on a new house at the moment... I was feeling in a rut, like nothing was moving or happening and all I do is go out to work every day. But you can still say you don't think it's a good idea to move without it being a personal attack on me in a public place. You brought up the BMW, but you are forgetting I had quite happily driven a 36-year-old Beetle since 1984; it was you who were unable to change gear. Did you mean all those things you said? I need to know whether or not you think all those things. x'

I didn't send it. Bunmi is really sick at the moment. The chemo isn't working and she keeps losing her balance. 'I have told her she is going to die,' The Husband says. 'She doesn't need people around her saying, "It'll be fine, don't worry"... She needs to face up to what is happening. We talk and talk and talk....'

Chapter 70

OCTOBER 10, 2004
HE CALLS ME A CLOTH-EARED BINT ON OUR
SECOND WEDDING ANNIVERSARY

We were on the plane to Marrakech to celebrate our second wedding anniversary. He was pretending to read a book about Al Qaeda. I started rummaging in my wash bag for lavender essential oil to put on my pulse points.

'Here, let me have a look,' he said, bored. How typical that he fished out the anti-cellulite gel and showed it to me.

'I told you not to be mean to me this weekend of all weekends,' I said.

'How am I being mean?' he asked, incredulous.

'You showed me the cellulite cream.'

'I see,' he said, unscrewing the top and taking a sniff. 'This stuff is like Kryptonite to you, is it?'

'For your information, I don't have cellulite. It's preventative.'

We had gone on our mini break with another couple, Clare and Alex, who were leaving their tiny baby, Apache, at home with her grandparents for the first time. They were being terribly lovey-dovey on the plane: canoodling, whispering, sharing bread rolls (The Husband stole mine).

We were met at the airport by camels and, although The Husband gave me a leg up, Alex wouldn't let Clare go anywhere near them in case she was bitten. The Husband got on another camel, and we swayed our way to the hotel in the desert, a 150-year-old restored fort with a spa! I looked back at him, to smile and wave, but he didn't look in my direction, merely looking really glum.

What a spoilt baby, I couldn't help thinking.

We got up the next day at 9 a.m. to go riding on beautiful Arab horses – they are really narrow, with dish faces and big eyes with long lashes – for three hours, and I know it was mean but I omitted to tell The Husband about the existence of the rising trot. That night, I put on my Dries van Noten dress and seventies Saxon vintage shoes (he wore his wedding tux, which was now several sizes too big) and we went for dinner by the pool. There was belly dancing and flamenco dancing. At ten past midnight, taking his cue from Alex, he started whispering in my ear.

'What, what? I can't hear you!' I shouted.

'I said, you cloth-eared old bint, Happy Anniversary!' (Needless to say, he hadn't got me a gift; as well as this weekend treat, I had bought him a lovely Helmut Lang wallet.)

That night in bed, after feeling very weird, I had to rush to the bathroom to throw up. Despite the fact my retching was very loud, and went on all night, hubby didn't stir. The next morning, he noticed that I was very pale and motionless. I then rushed to the loo again, shouting, 'Hold my hair! Hold my hair!'

On Sunday morning, I had to miss my rose-petal bath and aromatherapy massage, and he had to miss his quad biking in the desert, to catch the next flight home. In the airport, I had gone blind in one eye, and made very little sense (it was a migraine, something I thought I had left behind in my youth along with PVC lace-up boots and midi skirts).

We got home (I still had to drive from the airport) and our duvet didn't feel right. 'The dry cleaner has shrunk the duvet,' I told him crossly.

'Ah. They asked me to identify ours and I thought I had.'

I went to work the next day (at 4.30 a.m.) and left him a stern note: 'Please pick up the correct duvet and put on a clean cover.'

I rang the dry cleaner and primed them for his arrival. 'Whatever he says,' I told the dry-cleaning man, 'take no notice. He can't be trusted.'

I phoned home in the afternoon. I could hear the washing machine in the background.

'That's the duvet cover being washed,' he said proudly.

'Why didn't you just put on the spare one?' I asked.

'I didn't know we had a spare.'

'How can you possibly not know that?' I said in astonishment.

'Because I am not a woman,' he said, and put the phone down.

Chapter 71

NOVEMBER 28, 2004
HIS BASEBALL CAP PEAK JABS SNOOPY ON THE NOSE

I was telling my mum about the general naughtiness of The Husband, when she said, 'Darling, do you still love him?'

Do I? How do you know you are still in love with someone and not together because of three cats and the fact we have just had Sky+ installed. We all know what it is like to see David Cassidy for the first time in straining loons and a grandad shirt; that excited lurch in the stomach; a repressed scream in the throat; a warm glow. But I wonder if David and I had got around to discussing Snoopy's steroid tablet or the wet patch under the Smeg or the fact that our wheelie bin seems to have migrated across the road and been replaced by a much grubbier one, the allure of the cheesecloth might have palled somewhat.

Signs that mean I still love him:

1. When he sends me an email, I read it, close it down, and then, no matter how mundane the subject matter ('Chubby, Am off to yoga, and am recording Spurs and Channel 4 news on Sky+'), I will read it again, several times, throughout the day

2. I always read his star sign first. I have only just stopped doing that for Kevin (Aquarius), which must mean I have finally GONE OFF HIM.

3. When The Husband's name comes up on my mobile, I get really excited and sometimes drop it.

Signs I don't:

1. He phoned to say that Snoopy had just hissed at him and run away, completely out of character. 'What did you do to him?'

'I bent over to kiss him on his ears forgetting I was wearing a baseball cap, and the peak jabbed him on his nose.' He (The Husband) is now banned from wearing any form of headgear in the house.

2. Sometimes when I get home and his car isn't outside, I think, oh goody, pore strip, hair pack, oily bath ahoy!

3. Ummm...

So I am still in love with him. But the moot question is, does he still love me?

I send him a text, which takes about an hour as I am not very good at it. 'Sweetheart. Do you still love me, and if so, how can you tell? Urgent.'

His reply pops back. 'You're the one for me, Chubby. xx'

Chapter 72

DECEMBER 5, 2004
WE NEED TO TALK

All this week he has been at Bobby's cottage with his best friend Bunmi, her girlfriend Paula and their little boy, Remi. I sent a bike for the keys to the cottage, printed off a map, and arranged and paid for them to have dinner at The Place on Camber Sands on the Saturday night (David was going to join them). I, and I don't know why, was not invited.

Just before he left, I was having my marathon sleep when, at 9.15 a.m., he came and asked me a question about the route. All I said was, 'I'll draw you a diagram. I was asleep, by the way.'

And he replied, 'What's your problem?! You've got all day to sleep!'

I let that go, because Bunmi is so sick, but could have said, I don't actually, I have to go to work at 4 p.m.

It is now Wednesday. They are on their way back to London, and I have just received a text telling me not to bother with cauliflower cheese, as they are stuck in traffic. He had phoned me earlier, to ask me where the dustbins were. He had phoned me yesterday, in fact, and had sounded all quiet and distant, and I had asked him what was wrong, and he said, 'We need to talk.'

'Why, what? What about?'

'I can't talk now, there are people about. We'll talk when I get back.'

I hate it when men do this, try to be enigmatic and obscure. So tonight I drove home from work, my palms sweaty on the steering wheel, wondering what is in store. Are all relationships like this — from 'I luv u Chubby' to 'We need to talk' in a matter of days — or is it just mine? I thought once you were married they stopped playing hard to get.

Why, why am I such a pushover? I even went and bought milk and oranges today for him. It was so much easier being in love with Patrick Swayze.

We talk

He gets home. He had a nightmare journey. Bunmi was in so much pain she kept crying out when they went over speed bumps. Remi behaved so badly in the car he kicked a hole in the roof and chipped The Husband's tooth. He looks exhausted when he finally comes in the door. I go to bed quickly.

He gets in to bed. I put down my book, *A Sunday at the Pool in Kigali*, and give him a watery smile. He closes his eyes.

'I think we need to go into relationship counselling.'

'What for? Why?' I say stupidly.

'Because it is not working. You keep pretending. How can I know you when you don't even know yourself.' I tell him he has been distant for a year. That I feel I don't matter any more. That he avoids me but I have let it go because of his friend dying.

He guffaws. 'I've avoided you because all you ever do is bang on about work. What is it with you and your bloody job? I told Bunmi she makes less fuss about dying from cancer than you do getting up and going to the office. Why did you do it? What were you thinking?' His head is in his hands.

'Do what?' What have I done now?

'I was 26 when we met. My excuse is that I was young and stupid.

What was your excuse? You'd been through your twenties and thirties. What was wrong with you that you wanted to go out with just a boy, really. And telling me how old you were just two weeks before the wedding. What was I supposed to do? Call it off? The wedding invitations had all gone out. I have changed in the four years we have been together. If you were the same age we could have changed together. I'm embarking on what it is to be a man right now; you are about to embark on the menopause. I'm a different person to the one who asked you out.'

I am sure Guy Ritchie never says any of the above to Madonna. I tell him it is unfair for him to criticise my job when he has sat on his arse for most of the time. That I don't want to be with someone who could do that, see me leave at dawn every day and not lift a finger to help. I tell him that it is unfair to keep comparing me with Bunmi; that it's not my fault she is dying, but does he have to spend all his time with her, what about her girlfriend, her family, her sister, her friends? Does she know she has split us up? And why is he always bringing up his mother? If he is so worried about her cleaning job, why doesn't he get a bloody job, the lazy sod, so that he can give her money each week? She is not my mother. I have a mother whom I cook lunch for every week and give things to and phone every day. He accuses me of not wanting to get to know his culture (his very words were, 'How many gods are there in Sikh culture?' I don't bloody know), which I say is mean, as I am always the one saying, Let's go and see your mum, have you phoned her, why not get your baby sister to stay? I'm the bloody teetotal vegetarian in the family, not you, you fat fuck.

He started to cry, murmuring, 'When I came home last week, and I had just been with Bunmi to see the doctor, and he told her that he could do nothing more, all I wanted was for you to hug me and tell me you loved me but you didn't.'

No, I didn't. I had sat there with tears rolling down my cheeks. But I felt so excluded – from the weekend in the cottage, from visiting her in hospital – I assumed he didn't want me anywhere near him. Anyway, when has he ever comforted me?

I can't understand how we got to this point. Or if we are ever going to get past it.

Today, I was in the bathroom in an Eve Lom Rescue Mask.

'I do love you, you know,' he said, looking for somewhere unbesmirched to kiss my face. 'We'll always have a special place for one another, won't we?'

I don't want to have a special place. I want my life to be happy and normal. Why don't I deserve that? Did we ever really love each other? I remember when we first got Susie, and she was just a tiny scrap, and we put her in her basket in the spare room, and he went to tickle her head (she is very good at this now; she does a Stan Laurel impression) and she lunged and hissed at him and he, all 17 stone of him, leapt back with fear and banged his head.

'Oh, darling,' he said, 'I'm so sorry I frightened you.'

She is going to miss her giant dad.

Chapter 73

DECEMBER 24, 2004
THE LAST TIME WE HAD SEX

We are in bed. He whispers in my ear. I know he is up to something. He says he is going to break the rule. What rule? 'That I don't have sex with you because that would be unfair, that would make you fall more in love with me and think there's a chance that we are back together.' Oh for god's sake. Squeaky jumps off the bed. He smoothes the hair back from my forehead and I wonder if his hands are clean. He kisses my neck, great, slurping kisses, then he kisses my ear lobes. I don't want him to swallow my tiny bevelled diamond earrings I bought for myself so I manoeuvre him to my face. I am not a breast lady so he doesn't bother with those, he pulls my vest up and kisses my tummy and I squirm and he kneels on my hand Ow! and now he is manoeuvring his legs astride me he's much more bendy now that he does yoga how useful and then it is inside and he heaves and he leans on his elbows then I am on my knees and he is behind me and he comes and I don't.

Chapter 74

DECEMBER 26, 2004
LET HIM FIND SOMEONE WHO WILL TRAMP TO THE
POST OFFICE TO BUY HIS CAR TAX

Well, are we splitting up or aren't we? There have been a couple of signs that he is thinking of moving out, such as he has changed his mobile from contract (in my name, which I pay) to Pay As You Go, and he has suddenly started to look for freelance writing work. I have been trying to figure out where I went wrong. Have I let myself go? I no longer separate my lashes with a pin, but I still wash my hair every day, and condition it, and wear a clean T shirt and make-up, even at weekends. I have been thinking, will I ever be able to find someone else, given my past record? New Year's Eve is going to be like Millennium Eve all over again: four hours of TV and then bed. Still, I have lost my fear of being dumped, I just want it over with. Anything will be better than this, 'Is you Is or Is you Ain't?' It has been such hard work, exhausting! The constant, Are you okay? Shall we go to dinner? Shall I post this for you? Don't forget to renew your parking permit. Shall I book the hotel? I will print out directions. I will clear up. Don't bother, I will take Snoopy. And put the rubbish out. And on and on and on.

I ask him. 'What are you going to do?'

'I've ruined your life, haven't I. I do love you, but I just don't know…that might not be good enough.'

It isn't. Not by a long chalk. I think I am pretty special. Okay, I am not 25, but he wouldn't have liked me at that age, what with the leg warmers and the anorexia and the agoraphobia and the awful skin, and I had no money, no glamorous job. Nothing. Only my transient youth.

Let him find somebody else who will buy his car tax and stroke his fine black hair, like iron filings, until he falls asleep. I go back to my copy of Maggie O'Farrell's *The Distance Between Us* (excellent; full of unrequited yearning) and he is already sleeping the sleep of the innocent.

Chapter 75

DECEMBER 31, 2004
NEW YEAR'S EVE WITH LAST EVER EPISODES OF
FRIENDS, FRASIER AND SEX AND THE CITY

He has made no plans for New Year's Eve, but merely says, 'Would you mind if I went clubbing?' I say no. Then at about 5 p.m. when I say I want to go out to dinner because we've run out of food, he says, 'Have you booked a table?'

'No, I thought you would have booked.'

And he says, 'Well, I'm not that bothered.' He then goes to bed at 9.30 p.m. ('This Astanga yoga really takes it out of you. It was designed to be performed by warriors. It makes you really inhabit your own body, it opens you up. I feel much more open, that I want to be a nicer person') leaving me to have a baked potato with NOTHING IN IT. I watch the last ever episodes of *Friends/Frasier/Sex and the City* with Squeaky.

We go to visit Bunmi. She and Paula live in East Ham. I drive. She is upstairs, in a special hospital bed with lots of new pillows from John Lewis. She has gone blind in one eye. She has lost her hair, and a tube goes from under her scalp and into her belly. She cannot cross or uncross her legs. I offer her champagne. He sits with her on the bed and hugs her and kisses the top of her head in an intimate, gentle way he has never been with me. I drive to get us a Chinese takeaway. Her friend Helen from Brighton is busying about tidying things; they have been going over the funeral arrangements. I kiss her goodbye and I know I will never see her again.

Chapter 76

JANUARY 2, 2005
I GET TOWED

Something had to happen, didn't it? A catalyst, a pivotal moment. I drove to Islington to pick up some milk and some water, and as it was 5.30 p.m. and pouring with rain, I left my car for TWO MINUTES in a parking bay on a tiny side road outside the Italian deli, Monte's, while I dashed inside. When I came out, my car had vanished.

I phoned The Husband. 'I think someone's stolen my car, which is very annoying as my vintage shoes were inside.'

'Just let me finish this email and I will come and get you,' he said. 'My bet is you've been towed.'

Sitting in his Golf, I phoned the car pound. They had my car. 'It's your own fault,' he said.

'That's charming. All I want is a little sympathy. Like when you drove in a bus lane and got a ticket when you went swimming [both fines paid by me, of course]. It's not like I'm asking you to pay, I just want you to give me a lift.'

'I don't mind giving you a lift, I just can't bear to hear you banging on about it,' he said, making a movement with his hands to indicate me banging on. He then couldn't find his way to the Old Street roundabout. 'Shall I wait for you?' he asked as I flounced out the car. I slammed the door and didn't answer.

In the pound, waiting in line to pay my £200, I read the notice on the wall. 'When answering the phone to a driver, say your name, and good morning or afternoon, and then say, How can I help you? Ignore hot tears at all times.'

'All I can say,' The Husband said later when, finally, I stood dripping in the kitchen, 'is thank God we didn't adopt a child.'

I told him my mascara had run because of the rain, and I wasn't upset about the car, I was upset about his attitude, which was aggressive and unsympathetic (compare his reaction to my mum's, who when I told her said, 'Oh darling, can I pay the fine for you?').

'It's that whining tone in your voice – I can't stand it,' he said. 'And if you think I am aggressive, go on, find a man who is less aggressive than me.' And with that, he pulled off his wedding band and slammed it on the kitchen table, alarming Squeaky, who then padded it on to the floor.

'It's over,' he said.

'What are you going to do, move out?'

I have just heard the door to the spare bedroom slam. My first worry is that he will confuse Susie, who won't have access to her cushion. I don't understand why he is cross with me for being upset. Who wouldn't be upset? What am I, a robot? It seems that everything is fine as long as I creep about and pay the bills, but the moment I need him for anything, Shazaam, he is slamming things on tables and stalking off to the spare room. Now who is the baby?

Chapter 77

JANUARY 9, 2005
WHY DON'T I DATE A MAN MY OWN AGE?

How about Tom Cruise or Brad Pitt? Or Keanu Reeves? He's forty, although he does seem a bit moody, and he doesn't live in London. Or Mickey Rourke, except he has had all that plastic surgery and I don't think he would be very tidy. Of course, there are non-celebrity men over forty, I realise that. I suppose there is the odd one dotted around the office, but they are either married with hundreds of children, wear shiny suits and have old-lady arms, or are divorced and dating the blonde in accounts who catches a train in every day from Croydon.

I have to face it. When The Husband dumps me, which he surely will, I have to resign myself to being mummy to three very demanding cats. I might even get another cat. Or a horse. I could leave London and buy a minimalist farmhouse with stables.

What happened after he spent the night in the spare room? Well, the next day, he tried to act all normal, trying to hug me, which I didn't allow. Then he said, 'Shall we do something tonight?' and I said, 'No, I'm spring cleaning the fridge,' which I was. I kept forgetting to look at his left hand, but when I eventually did, he wasn't wearing his ring.

On Saturday, I asked him. 'Are you moving out or what? I need to get on with my life, make plans.'

'Well, I haven't moved out, have I?' he said. 'It is just that I am going through changes at the moment.'

'What's with the wedding ring? Have you lost so much body fat through yoga it keeps falling off? Has Squeaky swallowed it, or are we no longer married?'

'I don't want to be married any more. I know it is hard. It's going to be very painful not seeing Snoops every day, he's like a son to me. I don't regret these past few years with you; it has been fun, hasn't it?'

Do you remember that moment when The Husband (or The 26-year-old as he was at the time) stood in the doorway with his Charlie Brown face while I was on the phone to Kevin? I backed the wrong horse, didn't I?

JANUARY 23, 2005
PERHAPS YOU SHOULD GO AND STAY WITH DAVID

Friday. Up at 6 a.m. The Husband is at yoga. I feed all three cats (not as easy as it sounds, what with Snoopy's tablet and Squeaky's diet), strip bed, put on hot wash, lug bin bags to front of house, load dishwasher, have bath and iron white tuxedo shirt (£29.99 by Karl Lagerfeld for H&M; at last! I have discovered the high street). Shoot out door for 12-hour day, not a peep from The Husband, get home and repeat process, in reverse.

Saturday. Get up midday. He is at yoga; he is then going to see

Bunmi before a boys' night out.

Sunday. I cook my mum lunch; he watches Arsenal. That night, when I got home from mum's, he was on the phone, which, on seeing me, he took upstairs. I could hear him mumbling, 'I really need to talk to you about stuff.' Then, while I'm watching *Frasier* with Squeaks he popped his head round the door to say night night, and could I keep the noise down, at 9.30 p.m.

I pressed pause. 'What's going on?'

He sat down and rubbed his face. I told him what had been swirling around in my head, and he came over and tried to hug me and I gave him a big shove and told him he has until next weekend to decide whether or not he wants to be in a proper, grown-up relationship with me, which would involve talking and helping each other and sex and no secretive phone calls like a teenager. If he doesn't, he has to leave.

'But what if I don't know,' he wailed.

'Tough,' I said, pressing play.

The next day at work I received the following email:

'Thanks for being frank with me last night. I needed that. I had a deep think during yoga and realised I have never acknowledged how angry I am at what has happened with Bunmi. I am sad, yes, but also deeply bitter...and as the only people I spend any time with of late are you and Bunmi and Paula, it seems you are the one the anger was projected at. I am sorry. Have decided I need professional help to sort my head out, and will go into counselling before I do anything rash. Thanks for your patience. You've been brilliant. cccc'

Why the 'ccc's? Hmm. Counselling. Where have I heard that before? He never did get the number off Paula of a therapist and that was, what, back at the beginning of December? I sent him this:

'In two years I have never once complained or questioned the time you have spent with Bunmi, but I think she has drained you so much you had nothing left over for me. I have never once said you need to get a bar job to help fund your book, and it has been almost five years! We spent a year being interviewed about adopting and, without discussing it with me, you tell me you have changed your mind. Telling me I won't make a good mother was the most hurtful thing anyone has ever said to me. As I said last night, you have changed: you are so arrogant and selfish it is unbelievable! I still love you and would do anything for you, but the trouble is you know that and take advantage. I don't want to end up not liking you. The way you walked off with the phone mumbling was rude. I cannot take being ignored any more. I don't deserve it. I think it is a good idea you get help, but in the meantime, maybe you should go and stay with David. I am sure he would love to have you. You seem terribly unhappy at home.'

I received the following a few moments later:

'Susie fed; man been to view house; am off now to buy your parking permit. Wedding ring back on!'

Honestly.

Chapter 78

JANUARY 30, 2005
I'M TIRED BECAUSE IT'S FRIDAY!

Quick update. Ring back on his finger. He has just insured his car for another year, although I don't know whether this means he is staying or definitely going. He has tried to be more considerate. When he went to his mum's on Friday, instead of disappearing into a black hole, he phoned to say he wouldn't be home for dinner, and then started to give me advice on what I could have for supper. I stopped him when he started talking about chopping an onion. 'Oooh no, I don't want to do that,' I said.

'Why not, Chubby?'

'It would get the chopping board dirty, and I'd have to wash it and I might drop it again, and my fingers and the swing bin would smell of onion, then it would spit on the Smeg, and I'd have to wipe it and I'M TOO TIRED because IT'S FRIDAY!!'

It is a wonder he didn't leave me yonks ago.

Anyway, Susie still has a whole dad, Snoop and Squeak still have a step-dad and I still, in theory, have a husband. I said all of this to Kerry and she said, 'But do you think he is hedging his bets? Having an easy ride while not really ENGAGING with you?'

I told my mum he was behaving, remembering not to put my Myla knickers in a hot wash, learning how to switch the central heating on. 'I don't know, darling,' she said. 'I don't want you to get hurt. I was so lucky with Daddy.'

Anyway, today he has gone to visit his new female friend in Brighton. Strangely, I am not worried about this, which has set me thinking. At a party just before Christmas, he spent the whole evening talking to a rather stunning young lady who was easily young enough to have been my child if she hadn't been Vietnamese, and I remember thinking, See if she will put up with the fact you never shut drawers properly. I don't know if he will come home from Brighton tonight.

'What do you mean?' piped Kerry. 'I wouldn't have let Kevin go in the first place.'

Chapter 79

FEBRUARY 6, 2005
WE FIND EACH OTHER ANNOYING

Annoying things he has done/said recently.

1. He has started wearing trainers in the house; this is, he says, due to a head cold: the limestone floor in the kitchen exacerbates his symptoms.

2. He leaves the scratchy pad in the sink where it gets all soggy.

3. He keeps talking about the future in a way that doesn't include me, e.g. 'I'm thinking of going away for a while…' and 'I'm thinking of doing an MA…' and 'I'm thinking of getting tenure in New York.'

4. Over Christmas, he never once switched the tree's fairy lights on.

5. When he went to visit his new (female) friend in Brighton, despite phoning to say he was going to catch the last train back to London, he in fact didn't come home all night. He didn't apologise or explain, merely said it had done him good to wake up on a strange sofa and go out for a full English breakfast. Uggh. He didn't even take his toothbrush with him. I told him meat stays in the colon for up to SIX YEARS.

6. He leaves half-read books all over the house, but if I ever close them and put them on the shelf, he wails, 'But now I've lost my place!'

7. Peering at me this morning in bed, he said, 'You look much younger without make-up. Definitely under forty.'

8. He qualified the compliment, 'You've really lost weight,' with

the words, 'Are you trying desperately to keep me?' I told him I have probably lost weight because I am starving because he NEVER GOES TO THE SUPERMARKET!!!

9. Going back to the head cold, he blows his nose in his socks.

10. He keeps doing yoga.

11. He keeps eating sandwiches standing up, although he does have a plate.

I could go on, of course. But that would be very one-sided and not at all fair. And so I asked him to nominate all the things I do that annoy him, big or small. 'No,' he said, sitting cross-legged on the floor. 'I'm not going to go there.'

'No, go on, I don't mind.'

He paused. 'All right, then.

1. You always want to read in bed, when I want the light out.

2. When you get home from work, you are very difficult to be around, you go round dimming lights and demanding, 'Have you fed Susie?'

3. You always open things with your T-shirt. And you're always boiling J-cloths. It's like living with Howard Hughes.

4. You are always throwing my things away.

5. You are always terrified. Of losing your job. Of Susie being run over. Of losing me. And you're so needy…

Chapter 80

FEBRUARY 13, 2005
AM I BEING UNFAIR?

The Husband hasn't had an affair (at least, I don't think he has). He isn't an alcoholic. He doesn't gamble. Instead, he stands guilty of being too detached from me, not being sympathetic enough, leaving a tissue in with the dark wash.... Maybe I am being too harsh and demanding; perhaps I have watched too many episodes of *Sex and the City*. As Carrie would type at the beginning of an episode, 'Should I be expecting so much of the man in my life...?'

Let's take last weekend, with no comments/judgements/asides from me. Friday night, I booked a table for dinner. I got home from work. He'd had an awful day visiting B, who is in a lot of pain, and he thinks she is about to die. I said, Let's not bother going out, but he said, Yeah, let's go, so we did. I drove. He put on a good show for a bit, then he started crying. 'She is such a wonderful person,' he said. 'I'm about to lose the only person in the world who really gets me.'

After dinner, we walked to the car. 'Whenever I see Bunmi and Paula, they tell me I should do everything in my power to make things work between us,' he said, walking in a puddle.

'Really?' I said. 'But when you come home from being with them, or with David, you are really anti me.'

'Yeah, well, that's me, what I'm going through. All my friends really love you.'

On Saturday morning, I set off for a mini break. The Husband wanted to be on call for Bunmi, so I invited my sister along. We went to Babington House, and it was weird being there again, remembering how excited and in love I had been at our wedding just a few years ago. Then, I'd thought, It's finally, finally over, all those years of being single with no one around to put me first or to phone at six and say, What time are you coming home? But, arriving in Somerset this time, all I wanted to know was, Is our marriage finally, finally over?

'What would you miss about him?' my sister asked.

'Well, at first I thought I would miss the phone calls at work, the emails, the snuggles. But I don't have those any more. I'm tired of waiting for him to decide. I gave him an ultimatum and of course the deadline came and went and I did nothing. But I'm not afraid anymore, which is good,' I said, as we deposited our bags in our giant room, all floorboards and waffle bed linen and plasma screen. 'We're not going to last, I know that.'

As we drove back, thoroughly exfoliated, on Sunday night, I found I had a strange churning in my stomach. When I opened the front door, he shouted up the stairs, 'I'm making dinner.' He had put a wash on (although he had omitted to add soap powder), had spent the day following Susie around the house with a bowl of prawns, and he had taped all-new *ER*.

'Oh, and Celia from the cat home phoned,' he said. 'She said she has a lovely tabby kitten who might have brain damage, and do we want to have a look at her? And I said, "I'm not going to say I don't like the look of that one, of course we'll love her." Was that okay?'

FEBRUARY 20, 2005
I AM OFFICIALLY A MAD OLD CAT LADY

So, we have a fourth fur baby. I am officially a mad old lady with millions of cats. I had helped out at Celia Hammond's sanctuary in

East London a couple of weekends ago (v tiring; even though I told all the cats to sit nicely by their beds when I had finished cleaning their cages, as soon as my back was turned they were standing in their food bowls). Celia had told me about a little tabby who need-ed a home. I said I would get The Husband to come and see her; he had banned me from getting another cat, as he said he wasn't keen to be relegated to fifth, so I didn't mention it to him. But Celia was obviously insistent we have her, and had phoned him direct.

A few days later, he phoned me at work from Celia's. 'Lizzie, she's absolutely lovely,' he cooed down the phone. 'She's tiny, about three months, and she was rescued from a family who used to beat her about the head. So she's a bit brain damaged, and she has a hare lip, so her mouth makes the shape of an "Ooh", as if she's always about to say something, but I can't leave her here.'

That evening, I got home to find the new kitten, whom The Husband has named Sweetie, in his office. She can't stop purring. 'I'm going to sleep in here tonight,' he said. 'So she knows she's not going to be on her own.' Sweetie has a round little face, and is sur-prisingly trusting, considering her bad start in life. 'She's my cat,' he said, cradling her in his arms like a newborn. 'If I leave you, she's coming with me.'

I have to say The Husband is an excellent cat monitor. But, as usual, everything else has gone by the wayside. I sent him an email from work the next day:

'Darling, could you possibly replace the shower hose, which is broken, pick up my dry cleaning, and get some Super Floor clean-er. I will go to M&S to get cat food and organic chicken for Sweetie.'

I was going out for dinner with Jeremy that night. On the way there, I phoned home. 'No, I haven't been out today,' The Husband said cheerfully. 'I didn't want Sweetie to get bored. We've been watching telly.'

'Honestly,' I said to Jerry. 'He never does anything for me. I bought him a laptop for his birthday and gave him the wireless router and the airport thingy and broadband Internet access, and all I asked him to do was to connect my laptop as well. A year later and he still hasn't done it 'cos he can't be bothered. I'm at work 14 hours a day and I'm feeling overwhelmed. I get home and it's chaos: he's put a mug in the bathroom and his jeans are left where he stepped out of them. The swing bin is overflowing. I tell him I need tranquil surroundings and then he winds me up by saying he's going to take a picture of Susie with his new mobile phone and sell her on eBay. I can't stand it.'

Just then, my mobile phone rang. It was him. 'Lizzie,' he said, his voice cracking up.

'What's happened,' I said, alarmed. 'Has Sweetie gone up the chimney?'

'No. It's Bunmi. She has just died.'

Chapter 81

FEBRUARY 27, 2005
HE SAYS, 'WHY DO YOU ALWAYS HAVE
TO WATCH GRAND DESIGNS?'

Hmmm. What a week. I had decided not to do anything about our relationship until after Bunmi's funeral, which is tomorrow. Plus, on Tuesday, it was his birthday. (After much canvassing of friends, I bought him a mountain bike.) Despite the fact that he has been ignoring me and doing all the things he usually does, such as secreting mugs and leaving piles of clothes everywhere, I have been floating around in a Zen-like state, saying nothing. But then, last night, watching *ER* (during which he helpfully told me that the women he fancies most in the world are, in order, Alex Kingston, Kirstie Allsop from *Location, Location, Location*, Sarah Beeny from *Property Ladder* and Amanda from *A Place in the Sun*; you can tell from this list that, on the whole, I have jurisdiction over the remote control) he asked me if I still loved him.

'But that isn't in question,' I said.

'What is in question, then?' he asked, caressing Sweetie, who had inveigled her way on to his lap (she has settled in very well, by the way, although Susie is terrified of her).

'Whether or not you love me, and want to be in a relationship.'

'I never said I didn't love you,' he said.

'But it was implied. You said lots of mean things that basically made our relationship untenable. For example, that I am too old for you, that you don't want children, that you want to go away for a bit, that I don't know you, that I am closed, like a clam, that I'm dishonest, that you were young and stupid when you married me, that I'm too frivolous and lightweight...'

'I never said that last bit.'

'Yes you did, you said, why the oily bath, why do we always have to watch *Grand Designs*? You said you didn't know whether or not you wanted to be with me.'

'Yes, well. I didn't leave, did I?' (This a moot point. I emailed David about this, and he replied: 'I'm concerned that he is going to be out in the cold, knowing that he's blown it. He changes his mind like the weather and the one piece of consistency he's had in the past few years has been his relationship with you and the few close friends that can tolerate him! He's not the sort of guy who can deal with adversity, you know that. What's he going to do when you guys split? Where's he gonna go, back to his mum's place? C'mon… at his age? Can't you send him packing somewhere for a couple of months?')

I persevered, and told him he was being evasive. 'No, but nothing has changed. I'm still on tenterhooks. It's not fair.'

'Well, I love you enough,' he said, giving me Sweetie's head to kiss night night as he took her up to bed.

Oh dear. He loves me 'enough'. Well, I'm terribly sorry, but that isn't good enough. I want to be with someone who has a churning in his stomach when I call on the mobile. Who thinks about me all the time. Who would buy me a helmet and fluorescent armbands as well as a mountain bike. First, we have to get through tomorrow. Then, I have to tell him to go.

MARCH 6, 2005
HE SAYS HE HAS NEVER BEEN HAPPY WITH ME AND LYING ABOUT MY AGE TURNS OUT TO BE A VERY BIG DEAL INDEED

So, it's the evening of the funeral, and we've just got home. We're sitting on the sofa. 'That was a sad, beautiful day,' I say.

'You didn't lose Bunmi, I did,' he replies shortly.

We sit in silence for a bit and then he says, 'Do you really want to be a mum?'

'Pardon?'

'It's just I saw you holding that baby and you looked ten years younger [I hate it when people say that; it's like saying, 'You look well,' only much, much worse]. If you do, then we'll do it.'

'But we don't even know if we're going to stay together,' I say. 'You keep changing your mind.'

'The reason I changed my mind about adopting was that I thought I'd be home all day looking after it while you went out to work,' he says.

'That's weird. I thought I'd have to do everything, and you'd do nothing to help,' I say.

'Hmm, well, we need to talk more.'

So we do.

I find out that:

1. He hates being a husband; he feels 'unbelievable pressure' being married.

2. He was very unhappy and depressed for the first two years we were together; so much so he comfort ate.

3. For the past two years, he has had the attitude, I am going to do what I want, and if she doesn't like it she can kick me out.

4. He loves me.

5. He loves his new bike but was pedalling like mad and getting nowhere for ages and then yesterday he found out he could change gear.

6. He finds me 'emotionally distant and physically reticent'. I ask for an example. He says, 'Today, when I was feeling a moment of depression, my friend rubbed my back but you did nothing.' (I could have pointed out that I bought him a new suit for the funeral, paid for it to be altered, picked it up, ordered the flowers and picked them up, bought him a Helmut Lang tie, bought him a new Helmet Lang belt, took a day off work to go with him, polished his shoes.)

7. He always knew we wouldn't last.

8. He married me because he was 'in awe' of me (he isn't any longer) and wanted a nice lifestyle. He is 'really annoyed' I told him I was four years younger (it was actually three and a half) than I actually am (I'm really annoyed he lied about being vegetarian) and that he doesn't know any couples of such different ages who are even together, let alone in a successful marriage.

9. His best friend said that I was using him like a battery, feeding off him. I point out that one of us takes an afternoon nap, and it isn't me.

10. He thinks I married him because it heightens my kudos to have a young, handsome husband, and that all my female friends must be jealous.

He says he still wants us to go into counselling. 'If we can talk to each other as adults, then maybe we have a chance,' he says. 'Me saying I want to adopt a child with you, and be there for you both forever, means a lot. Much more than just saying I want to be married.'

'But don't you want a normal relationship, with someone who can have children with you? Who is too young to have owned a sweater dress?' (I didn't really say that last bit.)

'Who's to say I won't have that one day,' he says simply.

We are now in bed. 'Why don't you ever help me?' I ask him. 'I'm at work all day and you can't even change the cat litter or remember to buy dental floss. I'm busy at work and I might want to go for a swim at lunchtime but I always seem to end up in Marks & Spencer or bloody Boots.'

'I'll try to do more about the house,' he says, 'and I need to get a job, have my own income.... So. Do you want to try to make it work?'

I'm still reeling from the fact he has never been happy with me. We don't have a lot going for us, do we? I don't understand why he even wants to try. To be honest, I really can't be bothered.

Chapter 82

MARCH 13, 2005
I TELL HIM TO MOVE OUT

I went out for lunch with my friend Emine. 'How is he behaving?' she asked me innocently.

'Well. On Saturday morning I woke up at 9.30 a.m. feeling absolutely boiling, and wandered downstairs. For some reason the heating was on full and all the windows were shut. I opened the sitting room door and there he was, drenched in sweat, doing hot yoga. Susie was trapped in there with him looking very stressed, so I let her out, and then was on my way back to shut the door when it was slammed in my face. I opened it and asked him why he had done that, and he wouldn't answer; he was breathing, apparently, and just waved me away with his hand without looking at me.'

'No!' she cried. 'That's terrible!'

'Then,' I said, warming to my theme, 'later on I asked him if he was going to do any shopping and he said, "No, why?" so instead of going to meet my little friend Robi I had to go to Sainsbury's. That evening, I said I wanted to go and see *Closer*, and he said he had to have dinner first because he can't eat after 8 p.m. because of getting up early for yoga, and so we went into Islington, but there was a queue at the curry place, and he said he can't bear queuing for more than five minutes, and so we went to this really expensive Italian place that cost £70, and then he said he was too sleepy to go to the film.'

'You really have to get rid of him,' she said crossly. 'There is no point to boys at all unless they are being nice to you.'

He has been giving me mixed signals this past week. Having said that we must go into couples therapy, he has failed to get the number from Paula. Then he said that, this summer, we must to go Ibiza together to the yoga retreat he visited last year. 'You really need to start yoga at least three times a week,' he told me. 'You're really stiff, like a board.'

Then he said that if he gets lots of money for his book, he is going to 'arse around for a bit' and travel. 'What would you do if you had lots of money?' he asked me.

'I'd buy a horse and rescue chickens,' I said. 'And ducks.'

'Well, I think you should do that, but without me, of course.'

The final straw was when I asked him to do the garden, which now resembles a ploughed field. 'I'll pay you £500,' I said.

He thought about it for a few days, and then he said, 'The thought of doing the garden makes me come over all tired. I'm not doing it.'

So I tried a new tactic. Rather than nag him and whine, I just became silent and aloof. Last night, I got home and, ignoring his bike in the hallway, I took my supper upstairs and watched old episodes of *Moonlighting* with new puss Sweetie (she will eat anything: rice, couscous, pasta, cauliflower…If you take your eye off your plate for a second a huge, stripy paw will swipe something). After about half an hour, he appeared. 'Whassup, Chubby?'

'I'm just very disappointed,' I said. 'You spoiled my weekend, and then you wouldn't do the garden, for money.'

'Ahh,' he said, squirming around, batting his eyelashes. 'But I have a trump card. I know you'll never get rid of me because you love me.'

This morning, as I left for work at dawn, I asked him what his plans for the day were. 'I might go out and about on my bike, have lunch with my friend, then meet up with David to see a film. Then on Saturday, I'm going to see my mum.'

'That's fine,' I said. 'And when you see your mum, ask her if you can stay with her for a bit. I need some peace and quiet, when I can get up on Saturday and watch T4 without someone slamming doors. You're so annoying!'

He looked really shocked. 'Oh, okay, but for how long should I tell her I'll be there?'

MARCH 20, 2005
YOU DESERVE THE WORLD, AND WHATEVER
LITTLE BIT OF IT I CAN GET IS YOURS

I know I wrote that I said to The Husband calmly, 'Why don't you stay at your mum's for a bit. I need some peace and quiet'; and that he had replied, 'How long do you want me to go for?'

Well, I lied. That is not how it happened at all. It was much more fraught, more childish, silly, stupid.

I had got out of bed at about 2 p.m. and was sitting in an Eve Lom Rescue mask reading my Ian McEwan novel, drinking a cup of organic fair trade coffee, when he came in, breathless, pink from a hot shower. 'Lizzie, I'm really late. Could you give me a lift to the underground station?'

'Why don't you just drive?' I asked him, exasperated. 'I've just sat down, I've had a really busy week. I'd just like one day without having to drive.'

He looked really, really miffed. 'Well, thanks a lot,' he said. 'Don't ask me to do anything for you ever again.'

'Oh, so I don't do anything for you,' I said, thinking he's ruined my weekend again. 'I thought you were going to change the light bulb for me.'

'Well, I'm not going to,' he said, leaving the room and slamming the door.

I followed him. 'I want you to apologise,' I said. Silence. 'Fine,' I said. 'If you can't apologise, don't bother ever coming back.'

I went back in to the sitting room, and heard him moving around upstairs for a bit, and then the front door slam. I went up to the bathroom to see if he had taken his toothbrush, but it was still there. Still, I decided to have a clear out. I started with my desk, chucking out unopened bank statements and old bills. I found a little folded square of lined paper, with 'Lizzie' scrawled on the front. I unfolded it. I remember he gave this to me quite early on in our relationship. I probably shouldn't reprint it here, but it does show what we had, what we've lost for ever.

'I'm sorry for whenever I'm a chump,' he wrote. 'Terribly sorry. I've never been in a situation like this before, and I'm endeavouring to keep my mistakes to a minimum. I do, however, know that I love you. Your happiness makes me happy – and I caught myself smiling thinking about your smile (while I was emptying the bin). I want to be a writer. But I love you more than my dreams – so if ever you want me to get a regular gig, just let me know and I'll get one, because seeing you smile is worth everything to me. God only knows how much I love you. I want to be the man you've always wanted. Just tell me how. You are SO beautiful; so warm, so pure and SO decent. You deserve the world, and whatever little bit of it I can get is yours. I love you, N x

(Snoops and Squeaks send their love too xx).'

Chapter 83

MARCH 27, 2005
HE MOVES OUT, PART ONE

So. He spent the night at his mum's, with the words, 'And don't bother coming back, you're like a spoiled brat' ringing in his ears. He did come back, of course, the very next evening, although I still think 24 hours without brushing your teeth is not very nice at all. We didn't mention the previous day's argument, merely tip-toed around each other, and then, of course, on Monday morning, he went to yoga and I went to work.

But, and here is a surprise, the tables seem to have turned. I want him to leave, for various reasons, including the fact that he says he has never been happy with me, that he is far too young and will always make me feel old and aware of whether or not my upper arms have flaps or my elbows have weird baggy skin, and for the simple fact that he hasn't, for the past four years, been much of a friend, let alone a husband (what friend would make you go to M&S in your lunch hour just because they have been having a nap/watching *Eurogoals*?). I want to start a new life, without any-one bossing me.

But he, on the other hand, has suddenly become all loving and clingy. He keeps kissing me when he gets in to bed, and cuddling me (my usual response is 'Ouch, you are on my hair!'). He keeps saying he really, really loves me. That he is really grateful that I have been such a good friend to him. 'Why,' he murmured in bed to me last night, 'do you love me so much?'

'What do you mean? I don't,' I said.

'Yes you do,' he said, confused.

'No, I've gone off you,' I said. 'You've said too many horrid things. You are always bringing up how old I am. You've mucked me around. You're really lazy. You live your life as if I don't exist, always going out with David, leaving things on the table, you don't make a special effort when I get home.'

'Why don't you get rid of me, then?' he said.

'I have told you why. One, because you have nowhere to go, and two, because Bunmi was dying. But, now, I think it's time…'

'Yes, well, I feel all right now.'

'What do you mean? You've changed your mind, you want us to stay together?'

'Yes,' he said.

'Well, it's too late,' I said. 'I don't want to settle for second best. All my life I've dreamed about being in love, it's what has kept me going, really, and it wasn't anything like this. My dreams included Andrew McCarthy turning up to take me on a mini break, or Jan Michael Vincent arriving in a helicopter with a hamper [I can see from his expression that he has no idea who I am talking about]. I don't want someone who says mean things about me to his friends about me feeding off your energy. As if! I want someone who loves me like Jamie Oliver loves Jools, or…'

'Fine,' he said. 'If that's what you want. But you won't find another boy like me.' And with that, he started to pack his gigantic sports bag.

Epilogue

SO, WHAT HAPPENS, WHAT?

Chapter 84

APRIL 3, 2005
HE SAYS HE CAN TAKE OR LEAVE SQUEAKY

I can hear him crashing around upstairs. I am tempted to go up and supervise. I hope he takes that awful hooded sweatshirt. At least I will be able to put all my pristine copies of *Vogue* back on the shelves. I will have a nice, empty drawer for my linen sheets....

'Lizzie!' he shouts. 'Where have you put my rucksack?' He comes downstairs. He is cradling Sweetie and she is flailing her little legs, growling. 'I can't leave this little one,' he says. 'Or Snoops. Or Susie. Squeaky I can take or leave, really. I do love you loads. You know I've been feeling closer to you lately.'

I don't know. Aren't I putting off the inevitable day when he dumps me for someone more suitable, someone who has never owned a Wet Wipe, or a sweater dress? The meanest thing he has started to do lately is to feel my forehead and exclaim, 'Ooooh, hot flushes.' Ha bloody ha.

Are men worth the bother, the mess, the half-open drawers, the piles of coins, the constant yells of, 'Where's my...?'

'Who else would cook you great lentils? Who brought home Sweetie, and took Snoop to the vet when he tore his armpit?' he asks. He knows it is so easy to get round me.

I know we are unsuited. I know it will all end in tears, but I help him lug his enormous rucksack up the stairs.

APRIL 10, 2005
HE IS GOING TO BE A LITERARY SENSATION

I woke this morning to a cup of Illy coffee and two choccy biccies. He sat on the bed in his dressing gown and said, 'I feel completely happy for the first time in my life.' He tried to kiss me and the romantic moment – almost as good as when Nurse Hathaway went to find Doctor Doug Ross and he was on a jetty, and they kissed – was only spoilt by my Bliss Softening Socks. His mood has changed because yesterday, he sold his novel. After five long years. 'I'm going to be a literary sensation,' he said. I think I have underestimated how emasculated he has felt, living with me, old Miss Bossy Boots with her big salary and expense account and important meetings. I don't think New Man ever existed, not really. The Husband might brush his tongue, but he resented the fact that I held all the power in the relationship. Maybe that's why I chose him, because I didn't trust a man I couldn't control. It's that old 'I'm not worthy, I'm not worthy' voice squeaking away at the back of my mind: Why would a man pay to take me out to dinner?

LIZ JONES'S TOP 10 TIPS FOR A HAPPY MARRIAGE
   1. Never wear Bliss Softening Socks with Softening Sock Salve to bed. He will go off you.
   2. Never Mr Sheen the TV while he is watching the Milan derby.
   3. Give your husband his own personal space, even if it is just the cupboard under the stairs. Try not to Hoover his space. If he leaves

a rogue sock on the floor, try to ignore it.

4. Never refuse his conjugal rights. If you are feeling tired or bored during sex, try reading *Glamour*. I find it useful to talk to Squeaky.

5. Remember, men are like goldfish: you must never overfeed them.

6. Never say he just has a cold when he is clearly suffering from a debilitating strain of flu.

7. You have to become Superwoman. You must always go shopping at lunchtime and remember to put out the recycling box and buy the four-in-one dishwasher tablets.

8. Never, ever ask him to do something while he is doing something else.

9. You must develop the skills of a bloodhound, able to track down missing objects – wallet, mobile phone, baseball cap, passport – in moments.

10. You must say, 'Don't worry, I'll do it,' at least a million times a day. Do not make him sit on the naughty step. Remember, you are not his mother.

APRIL 24, 2005
IT IS THE FIFTH ANNIVERSARY OF THE DAY WE MET

We were in bed last night when he said, 'Today was the fifth anniversary of when we first met'.

It must be said we have had our fair share of ups and downs.

Ups
  • The night I found Susie in the Wendy House.

• The day he brought home Sweetie, her mouth in a permanent, 'Ooooh!'

• The day he got his book deal and said he was going to make sure his mum never had to work again.

Downs

• The day I told him how old I was and he pranged the BMW.

• The day he said, 'I've never been happy with you. When we first started going out you were a complete cow.'

• The day we got back from honeymoon and I couldn't get the aforementioned BMW out of the long-term car park.

• The day he told me he had slept with someone else soon after we started going out. He said he hadn't really fancied her, but did it because he was 'on a roll'.

• Our wedding. Let's face it: it was stressful. I hated my hair. The manicurist made my fingers bleed, which made a smudge on my outfit. I have never framed the wedding photos.

• The day Snoopy got pancreatitis.

• The day he said, 'My friend Bunmi makes less fuss about dying from cancer than you do about getting up and going to work.'

• The day Bunmi died.

• The day I finally got the approval letter from the adoption people and hid it in a drawer.

'It's been fun, though, hasn't it?' he said, trying to hug me with Squeaky's big bulk wedged between us. 'My friend Julie says that when I get the cheque for my book I should take you out to dinner.'

'She did, did she?' I said flatly.

'Yes, but I said I was going to take you on a mini-break instead. I wouldn't have been able to write the book without you, Chubby.

I've already started the next one. Do you want to hear the opening sentence?'

MAY 8, 2005
CREPUSCULAR IS NOT ANOTHER WORD FOR CELLULITE

We had a really long talk last night. It was five past 11 and I was just switching off *Sex and the City* when he came and sat next to me on the sofa. My fear of him doing this sort of thing has diminished somewhat with frequency, so I just sat calmly, thinking I must get to bed, as I have to be up early. He was staring at Bunmi's photo on the mantelpiece. 'I think about her every day,' he said. 'We were so close. I used to say to her, "Who will I talk to this deeply when you're gone?" I think having gone through this with her has made me a nicer person. I've grown up a lot. In those months leading up to Christmas it was like everything was exploding, and my life was falling apart....'

Then he started talking about how she introduced him to yoga (she didn't; I did, I sent him to Ibiza on a yoga mini-break!) and about truth being a platform, and the nature of fear.

I have yet to receive an apology for being hit by that explosion; surely if he said all those things – that I'd be a terrible mum, that he's never been happy, that I made him depressed – he must have meant them, at least on some level. He keeps talking about himself, how he is feeling, but we never talk about me. I don't care about 'the nature of fear'. All I know is I've spent most of my life experiencing it. I am tired of not being good enough. He is always gleefully pointing out my malapropisms. For example, the other day he was leaning over my shoulder reading a piece I was writing about a new spa, and he burst out laughing. Apparently, crepuscular is not another word for cellulite. Big bloody deal. I am beginning to think being single would be so much easier, so much less work. Instead of lying flat on a pillow, he punches it and scrunches it up and folds it and then he puts his head on it? Why?

MAY 15, 2005
I THINK I JUST WANT HIM TO GO AWAY
AND LEAVE ME ALONE

Would I be happier being single? It's just that being married is SO exhausting. The Husband never goes to the supermarket; even when I email him a shopping list to order on Ocado he just doesn't do it. Consequently, on Saturday I found myself going to all these bijou shops in Islington (I draw a line at Sainsbury's on my day off) and spending £7 on a TINY bag of handmade granola (his fault, obviously) while he sloped off to Triyoga in Primrose Hill. The final straw was when I caught him dipping his finger into my Sisley All Day All Year cream, which cost £150. 'You spent £150 on this?!' he exploded. 'It protects me from free radicals,' I replied smugly.

Take Sunday. He disappeared to yoga, again, at 8 a.m., having asked me quite loudly about Snoopy's tablet, and I didn't hear from him until 17.38 (I have just consulted my text message inbox), when he wrote: 'Had lunch. Sobering up with coffee. Be home soon. xx'

Then on Monday morning I emailed him, saying I would like to see the new film about Hitler, and he sent this reply:

'Don't want to watch film about Hitler; want to make vegetable korma and have night in. All tabbies re-fed; Susie shut in lounge with brekkie. Am going to finish revision of my novel today, and begin new book tomo. Go swimming tonight; v.good for you... xx'

That email made me quite cross, actually. He only wants a night in because he has been out all weekend. I haven't been anywhere. Fine that he has fed the pussies, but I don't think I can stand another five years of him writing a novel on the kitchen table. And I hate swimming. The pool makes my hair go green, and no matter how hard I try, I always stay in one place, spluttering. And what is he implying by saying it will be good for me? What?

Take what happened on Wednesday. I had invited best friend Kerry round for supper to meet Sweetie, and I said to The Husband that I would order a veggie curry. 'No, no,' he said, 'I will go shopping and cook my famous vegetable tagine.' Wednesday dawned, and I emailed him from work with a shopping list. I phoned at 3 p.m. No reply. I phoned at 6 p.m. No reply. Maybe he's left me, I thought. I phoned at 7.20 p.m. to tell him I would be late home and that he would have to entertain Kerry for half an hour. I was just leaving yet another message when he picked the phone up. 'I went for a nap at 2.30 p.m., and have only just woken up,' he said groggily. 'So I didn't get any shopping, or fizzy water, or cat food. Could you order the takeaway as you are driving home?'

Last night, we were in bed when he started hugging me. He said he was feeling happy and thinking straight for the first time in months. He then actually said he was 'sorry' for having put me through the past year or so. 'Even when I was being mad and horrid, you still loved me,' he said. He then asked me how I was feeling. Blimey. I told him I wasn't sure, which is true: I'm not. Most of the time I just feel exhausted. I think I want him to go away and leave me alone. 'Are you feeling scared, glum?' he asked helpfully.

'Not scared, but sad. Disappointed.'

'About what?'

'About us. How it's turned out. It hasn't been like I imagined it would be. I thought we would have had more fun together, that we would have shared more. I don't know about you, but I took our wedding vows very seriously. I put you first, even before me, if not quite before the cats. I want to be the most important person in your life. You said once that you had ruined my life, and in a way yes, that's true. Don't you care that I'm unhappy? You want us to split up, remember.... It has all been one big, fat failure. We've only been married for two years. It's pathetic.'

There were a few moments before he said, 'I certainly don't want us to split up right now. Far from it.'

'But we haven't resolved anything.'

'All I can say is that when I wake up in the morning I will love you, and when I go to bed tomorrow night I will go to sleep loving you. I can't say fairer than that, can I?'

THE END

ACKNOWLEDGEMENTS

With thanks to Jeremy Langmead, Katharine Viner
and Sue Peart for commissioning me to write
about my life in the first place. Huge thanks to
Kerry Smith, Hannah Pool, Amy Wilson,
Veronica Wadley, Georgina Capel and Robert
Caskie, Julie Burchill, Bee Murphy, Nicki Marshall,
Ros Holder, Clare Lattin and Jane O'Shea.